MINA LOY

MINA LOY
APOLOGY OF GENIUS

MARY ANN CAWS

REAKTION BOOKS

Published by
REAKTION BOOKS LTD
Unit 32, Waterside
44–48 Wharf Road
London N1 7UX, UK
www.reaktionbooks.co.uk

First published 2022
Copyright © Mary Ann Caws 2022

The right of Mary Ann Caws to be identified as Author of this Work has been asserted by her in accordance with the Copyright, Designs and Patents Act 1988

All rights reserved

No part of this publication may be reproduced, stored in a retrieval system or transmitted, in any form or by any means, electronic, mechanical, photocopying, recording or otherwise, without the prior permission of the publishers

Printed and bound in India by Replika Press Pvt. Ltd

A catalogue record for this book is available from the British Library

ISBN 978 1 78914 554 0

For permission to quote from Mina Loy's published writings, grateful acknowledgement is made to Roger Conover, Mina Loy's editor and literary executor; Farrar, Straus & Giroux; and the Jargon Press on behalf of the Estate of Mina Loy. For permission to quote from Mina Loy's unpublished writings in the Mina Loy papers at the Beinecke Rare Book & Manuscript Library, the publisher wishes to thank Yale University, Roger Conover and the Estate of Mina Loy. All writings by Mina Loy © 2021 by The Estate of Mina Loy.

'Notes from Underground: W. H. Auden on the Lexington Avenue IRT' from DAYS OF WONDER: *New and Selected Poems* by Grace Schulman. Copyright © 2002 by Grace Schulman. Reprinted by permission of Houghton Mifflin Harcourt Publishing Company. All rights reserved.

Quotations from the letters of Joseph Cornell © 2021 The Joseph and Robert Cornell Memorial Foundation / Licensed by VAGA at Artists Rights Society (ARS), NY.

CONTENTS

Introduction: Why Mina Loy Now? 7
1 London and Munich, 1882–1900 14
2 'Parturition': Paris, Florence, New York, 1900–1916 21
  Interval: Futurism 36
3 Diversions, 1914–53 63
4 New York and the Arensberg Circle 76
  Interval: Arthur Cravan 90
5 'The Widow's Jazz': Paris Again 115
6 *Insel*, 1933–6 122
  Interval: Mina Loy the Artist 131
7 New York Again, 1936–53 166
8 Aspen, 1953–66 180
9 Always Ample Space 195

REFERENCES 199
SELECT BIBLIOGRAPHY 209
ACKNOWLEDGEMENTS 211
PHOTO ACKNOWLEDGEMENTS 213
INDEX OF WORKS BY MINA LOY 215
GENERAL INDEX 218

Mina Loy, c. 1905, portrait photograph by Stephen Haweis.

INTRODUCTION: WHY MINA LOY NOW?

Mina Loy the painter and poet was desperately, irretrievably and movingly modern. She performed in her prose, both theoretical and autobiographical, and her poems, an astonishingly complex mingling of the mental, the physical and the scientific, the most forward-looking feats imaginable. Her various forms of art, from the decorative to the painterly and abstract, spread out over places and genres both expected and unlikely. All through her life and its ventures, Mina Loy knew how to craft a singular and object-filled life. She was in one person a multi-flavourful assortment, a highly colourful modernist being.

After attending art school for the first time in London, she moved to another in Munich, and then to Paris, where she and a friend attended the Académie Colarossi at 10, rue de la Grande Chaumière, studying under Whistler. In a night class in drawing, she met the photographer and artist Stephen Haweis, who became her first husband and the father of a child who died very early on. Recovering from that loss, Mina was helped by a kindly and elegant physician, Dr Henri Joël Le Savoureux (delightful name – who was, alas, engaged to another), with whom she had her daughter Joella. Stephen was eager to move to Florence; there, in a grand villa just outside the city in Arcetri, lived the larger-than-life personality Mabel Dodge, an American hostess on a grand scale, then patroness of the Armory Show and columnist for the Hearst organization. Through Mabel Dodge, Mina met the editor Carl Van Vechten, a more than problematic character who was constantly helpful to her writings, and Gertrude Stein, about whom Mina wrote several times. She read a poem about Stein (originally published in the *Transatlantic Review* in 1924), calling her 'Curie/ of the laboratory/ of vocabulary', at Natalie Barney's famous Temple de l'Amitié at 20 rue Jacob.[1] The famous and beautiful lesbian writer presided over this salon in her white dresses with her golden-blonde hair, a ladykiller supreme. There Mina also met the painter Frances Simpson Stevens, with whom she encountered the Futurists in Florence and Milan. She rapidly became involved with both the colourful and stagey Milanese Filippo Tommaso Marinetti and the more traditional Florentine Giovanni Papini.

After leaving Florence and her Futurist life, Mina Loy left for New York, where her friend Frances Simpson Stevens helped her settle and introduced her to the Arensberg Circle. In Walter and Louise Arensberg's duplex apartment at 3 West 67th Street she was to encounter the proto-Dada Arthur Cravan, whom she had seen at the opening of the Society of Independent

Arthur Cravan, c. 1913.

Artists Exhibition on 18 April 1917 at Grand Central Palace, where her painting *Making Lampshades* was exhibited. The next day Cravan was to lecture there on 'The Independent Artists of France and America', but arrived drunk, thanks to the ministrations of Picabia and Duchamp preceding the performance. Thereupon he removed his coat, waistcoat, collar and braces, began to shout obscenities and was hauled off to a police station.² On 25 May Mina and Cravan attended the Blindman's Ball in Webster Hall, and the next day he gave a lecture and disrobed, as he had done previously.

In keeping with his frequent travelling habits, Cravan left New York, deluging Mina with letters from elsewhere, and then journeyed to Mexico to teach boxing. He wrote from there in December to beg her to join him, which she did. There they married and wandered around, poverty-stricken; they planned to escape from the port Salina Cruz to Argentina, hoping for better times. Mina was to leave on a passenger ship for Buenos Aires, and Cravan was trying out a small boat heading for Puerto Angel. But he never returned to Salina Cruz.³

There are many stories about his mysterious disappearance, all of which position him as the diametrical opposite of Haweis, Mina's first husband. One absolute fact is that he was the nephew of Oscar Wilde, as whom he liked posing and about whom he tells a grand and impossible tale of a visit: 'Oscar Wilde est vivant!'⁴ Another sure thing is that he was Mina's passionately adored lover and second husband, her 'Colossus', the father of her daughter Fabienne, after his birth name: Fabian Lloyd. He was the editor and author of many parts of the six numbers of the splendidly peculiar literary review *Maintenant*, and was himself a bizarre compilation of boxer, writer, editor and a number of other occupations, before his mysterious and much-discussed appearances and disappearance. He was spectacular in every imaginable way and some that are unimaginable.

This was Mina's lifelong loss. She was, after this Dada encounter, no less a Surrealist personality, unfixed in place between Paris and London and New York again; finally she lived in Aspen, Colorado, with Joella and Fabienne, where I went to follow in her tracks. Most interesting to me, apart from the zigzags of places in which she lived and the so variously motivated and arrayed personalities with whom she was involved from near or far during her lifetime, are her poems. She claimed not to be a poet – why is anyone taking an interest in my poems?, she queried, and indeed for a very long period wrote none at all – but I found her poems mesmerizingly present. They instigated the present book from the beginning, informing its various parts, interweaving with her life as much in their texture as in their envisioning of all her twists and turns from Futurism to Dada, Surrealism and Christian Science.

Ezra Pound, the premiere of whose opera *The Testament of Villon* Mina Loy attended in 1926, claimed that it was her 'logopoeic' handling of abstract vocabulary that made her satirical style so distinctive.[5] Most arresting among so many other facets of her poems is the way in which the various beads of elements in them – whether early and satirical or later and impassioned in their details and overall ideas – glitter and often oddly find themselves next to each other. We are often uncomfortable making our way between them, and seldom is there an overall impression: we are left suspended. I find this especially captivating in the reams of unfinished, incomplete poetic texts she left behind, many of which are gathered in the Beinecke Library

Introduction: Why Mina Loy Now?

Portrait photograph of Arthur Cravan impersonating Oscar Wilde, 1913.

at Yale, together with the abundant prose. For this reason, among others, my writing will focus mainly on her poetic texts, in poems and in prose. This book will not address her artwork, except in passing. A serious study of Mina Loy the artist is long overdue. An exhibition scheduled to open at the Bowdoin College Museum of Art in 2023 will mark the first serious attempt to address this long-neglected subject.

Why is she so often compared to Marianne Moore, who to me seems so very different? Moore's control of the text does not make me uncomfortable – she feels in charge. And I think I know where she is going, and I can go along or not. With Mina Loy I am never sure where she is or isn't going, and don't really feel either invited or excluded: I am not sure she knows I am there. These separate spectacular gems have no concern for the reader. Easier by far is the identification of various personalities in her text, such as the Futurists she was involved with, the explosive and colourful Filippo Tommaso Marinetti of Milan, or the far less dramatic and scene-conscious Florentine Giovanni Papini: one can often recognize these figures in the titles of the texts. Mina herself is recognizable only in her brilliant variousness. Tara Prescott found her work 'layered and confounding'.[6] Of herself, Mina Loy said: 'Speak-easy? Why, if I ever tried to speak easily some policeman would come up and give me a really hard sentence!'[7]

She perfectly suited her times, as did her costumes. Magically, she made an instantaneous, intuitive adjustment to whatever situation she inhabited. This is in no way to suggest that, living in the Lower East Side of New York City, mingling with the Bowery bums who took to her as she did to them, she would always wear shabby clothing. True, she ended by wearing her nightgown outdoors to appear with them, and they always found her saintly, no matter what clothes she appeared in. Her very changeability suited her well. We, her readers and very much aftercomers, can follow her from the early garb to the later, and from her early art in its peculiar Mannerist and Gothic mode, and her poetry from its early stages, its mockeries and flounces, through the salon conversational mode, to the Cravan-oriented lamenting and wandering modalities and the Bowery musings on the angelic bums, and on to the mental-metaphysical Christian Science texts, and the intermingling with Joseph Cornell boxes and arrangements, and her own pre-Schwitters constructions from found objects.

There is absolutely no way even the most easily diverted readers can find themselves bored with Mina Loy: it is rather as if she had almost as many personalities and various expressions in various genres as Fernando Pessoa (1888–1935), the astounding Portuguese master of the many, including eighty or so literary alter egos, who wrote in Portuguese, French and English.[8] Mina Loy, fluent in German, French, Italian and English, is as influential in contemporary writing these days as Pessoa, both of them writers of genius. We are, at our best, reading, looking at and listening to Mina right now.

1

LONDON AND MUNICH, 1882–1900

Mina Loy, born Mina Gertrude Lowy, was the first of three daughters. Their parents were Sigmund Felix Lowy, a tailor of Hungarian Jewish heritage, and Julia Bryan, a British Methodist. The mother, judgemental in every way, became the voice resounding negatively in her eldest daughter's ears.

The tenseness in their marriage, between a foreign Jew and an antisemitic Christian, gave birth to the long and celebrated poem *Anglo-Mongrels and the Rose* (1923–5). The rose represents the uptight British mother, while the father, 'Exodus', lapsed into hypochondria by the 1890s.

> Exodus knows
> no longer father
> or brother
> or the God of the Jews
> it is his to choose
> finance or
> romance of the rose[1]

The coupling of this lower-middle-class Christian and the Jewish highest-paid tailor's cutter in London, now called a draper, was not a success, for they were desperately different:

> She
>   simpering in her
>   ideological pink
> He
>   loaded with Mosaic
>   passions that amass
>   like money
>
>   implores her to take pity   upon him
>   and come and be 'a Lady in the City'
>   ...
> For in those days
>   when Exodus courted the rose
>   literature was supposed to elevate us[2]

They had an uneasy time from the beginning. See a section of the poem entitled 'Opposed Aesthetics', and another, 'Marriage Boxes', which gives us the general idea. From Julia's point of view, as mirrored complexly in this long poem, the sexual and blood relationship is a terrific indictment of the flesh.

> Oh God
> that men and women
> having undertaken to vanquish one another
> should be allowed
> to shut themselves up in hot boxes and breed

spirits of prey
ceaselessly
on the watch in their cruel privacy

Seizing upon occasion
for crippling the personal

to test the law of the craftiest for survival[3]

The young Mina did not take to the idea of the hot box, or to the idea of having to hold her tongue, and did not do so. Everything she wrote at every important poetic point in her life worked against tameness and calmness, and towards that immensity and intensity we so admire in her.

Mina was called a 'goy' by her father, whereas her Protestant mother wanted to shuffle her off on to her father. There were endless battles over propriety; equipped with her doll, Mina would favour the left side and make faces at the right, always being on the side of the underdog. This concurs with all her poems about the Florentine slums, as well as the epic poems about the New York Bowery and other glum quarters.[4]

Just as procreation was a forbidden topic to the uptight Methodist mother, Julia, all erotic art seemed to be immoral, so that, as Carolyn Burke points out, the paintings she preferred had no legs, whereas the other parts of the body were linked just by the clothes.

It all fits: the artist Kate Greenaway was their neighbour in Hampstead, with her innocent-beyond-belief young girls and the patterns of their dresses. This atmosphere played into the delicate pictures by Mina Loy as a young artist, full of cupids and swans and cherubs, where the decorative easily glides over the meaningful, and surface prettiness apparently presides. On the superficial level, I would link this to the seeming attraction of words and sounds over meaning, as Ezra Pound points out, and, again superficially, of the importance to her of clothing and her appearance. Nurses and governesses came and went. Later, a religious companion, Lilah, was dismissed, and a new nurse, Queenie, walked the child Mina around the neighbourhood. Later still came Miss Ware, a strict disciplinarian, and Miss Nickson, devoted to religious studies, whose physical appearance reminded Mina Loy of a pig. Her artistic sight was always sensitive, as was her entire being.

Mina was permitted to attend art school; not the Slade, but 'the Wood', founded in 1878 in St John's Wood. She would take the bus down the Finchley Road, past cottages and, on Grove Road, the famous homes of James Tissot and Sir Lawrence Alma-Tadema. In her art studies she was drawn to the Pre-Raphaelites, to whom Quentin Bell attributed a 'mournful aesthetics . . . a world in which no violent emotions existed, in which everyone is quietly and decently sad'.[5] Sad and mad: we are imagining Max Nordau and his thought of their moral debasement, as in his 1839 book *Degeneration*. Mina was especially attracted by Dante Gabriel Rossetti: 'How could a man named more ornately than other men be mad?'[6]

As opposed to the delicacies of the Pre-Raphaelites, the Lowys leaned towards heaviness in all domestic realms: heavy furniture, overstuffed chairs, gilded mirrors, ebony and alabaster. All of this was opposed to Mina Loy's longing for a sense of mystery, and her artwork of this period. She would paint or draw white swans and a cupid sitting on their white feathers, or a bronzed cupid against the fan of a peacock. She would read Ouida, and her mother would take the book away and place it under lock and key. Julia's 'middle-class morality', as Burke so perfectly terms it, would have no room for any sensational tales or the temptations that would surely be prevalent in a place like Paris, with its demi-monde women and its excessive freedom. Even the less reputable parts of London were supposed to be dangerous, since Mina might be taken for an actress – or worse. When Mina wrote a poem about the marriage of a daisy and a gnat – which seems fairly innocuous to us, the readers – Julia advanced the idea that her daughter had the mind of a slut. So much for the physical part of marriage, clearly abhorred in Mina's epic poem *Anglo-Mongrels and the Rose*.

In 1892 her father bought them a home at 68 Compayne Gardens, in a newly developed part of West Hampstead. Mina Loy reserved for herself in this area she called 'Clinton' a few private places, which she endowed with some brand of her 'curative colour', much as Japanese paper flowers spread out miraculously when you place them in water. At the time she entered art school, her father decided that the Jewish sound of Lowy was too embarrassing, and her name was changed to Loy. Then, by another kind of miracle, she was allowed to attend the Münchner Künstlerinnenverein – the Society of Female Artists' School in Munich – which was respectable in every way. There, she was sent to live at the household of a baron and baroness, the latter calling herself Mammalie, who was as affectionate towards Mina as her mother was not. (Burke does not name the baron and baroness, which seems absolutely right: they represent rank and respectability beyond any individual names.) Mina's family had sent £300 to the baron and baroness for an

Mina Loy as a student.

evening gown for Mina, so she could go out in proper society with a chaperone, but she found they had used the funds on their holiday to see the Passion Play, only put on every ten years. The baron and baroness expected her to flirt with young men, but Mina adopted velvet knickerbockers and a pipe; 'safely unchaperoned', she frequented restaurants, music halls and studios in her performing self as it developed.

Her first teacher in Munich, Maximilian Dasio, specialized in mythological paintings and inculcated in his students a great respect for draughtsmanship, which never left Mina. Nor did her appreciation of the 'applied' arts, which by 1900 were exhibited on an equal status with 'fine' art, so that Mina came to admire the lamp designs in iridescent or opaque coloured glass that would be such a part of her later designs. There was no more split between high and low art, and Mina would incarnate this lack of distinction for her entire life.

Speaking German, she began to be called 'Dusie', as in the informal *du* and the formal *Sie* of the German language, which she used interchangeably. She revelled in the carnival season, with its masqueraders tossing out confetti, and exulted in a new kind of freedom. Dining in outdoor restaurants, spending hours on barges and in rooftop studios, she closed out this year of her life before returning to London and then to Paris.

Of the years between Munich and Paris, Mina is said to have observed ironically: 'I went home to England and stayed there a few minutes.'

2

'PARTURITION': PARIS, FLORENCE, NEW YORK, 1900–1916

Mina felt powerless upon her return home. Her father's nervous hypochondria worsened, along with her mother's judgemental temperament. Mina felt close to her sister Dora, far less so to the youngest sister, Hilda; Julia had forbidden her to play with Hilda, to keep the younger daughter free from moral taint. To lessen the hostilities at home, Mina was allowed to board with a friend, Eva, and her mother, Mrs Knight, who, appreciating her drawings, permitted her to smoke cigarettes. Mina was able to join them in Paris and attend an art school there, boarding with a friend.

By this time, women were allowed to attend the same art classes as men. At the Académie Colarossi on 10, rue de la Grande Chaumière, Mina was peculiarly attracted by a young art student from a privileged family. The son of a parson, Stephen Haweis (whom she was later to call Esau Penfold) was short with dark hair and an Oxonian accent; he dressed outlandishly, with dangling necklaces and sporting a red sash. Haweis was a photographer (he made some wonderful portraits of Mina) as well as a painter. At 21, finding herself pregnant with his child, Mina entered into a marriage with 'this dark-haired dwarf', a union that never went well.

Stephen Haweis, *Sea Garden*, c. 1918, oil on canvas.

Mina's extraordinary talent for fashion manifested itself, as did Stephen's for photography. He had studied painting with the great Czech artist Alphonse Mucha and had taken up photography with another Englishman, Henry Coles, whose firm (aiming at 'something like the quiet harmony and balance of Whistler's painting') photographed Rodin's sculptures. Stephen delighted in his beautiful wife and model, and in his connections to the art world, dining with George Moore and Walter Sickert, befriending Eileen Gray, and frequenting Colette and Willy, and Carrière.

'Dusie' (Mina nude), Paris, c. 1905, photograph by Stephen Haweis.

Parturition

Mina had a difficult labour, during which Stephen visited Amelia Defries, a woman Mina assumed to be his mistress. Her poem of ten years later, 'Parturition', expresses the almost inexpressible pain of giving birth in the very 'nucleus of being' even without the consciousness of a betraying husband:

> I am the centre
> Of a circle of pain
> Exceeding its boundaries in every direction
>
> The business of the bland sun
> Has no affair with me
> In my congested cosmos of agony
> From which there is no escape
> On infinitely prolonged nerve-vibrations
> Or in contraction
> To the pin-point nucleus of being
> . . .
> The open window is full of a voice
> A fashionable portrait-painter
> Running up-stairs to a woman's apartment
> . . .
>   The irresponsibility of the male
> Leaves woman her superior Inferiority
> He is running up-stairs
>
> I am climbing a distorted mountain of agony
> Incidentally with the exhaustion of control

I reach the summit
And gradually subside into anticipation of
Repose
Which never comes
For another mountain is growing up
Which   goaded by the unavoidable
I must traverse
Traversing myself

. . .

There is a climax in sensibility
When pain surpassing itself
Becomes Exotic
And the ego succeeds in unifying the positive and
    negative poles of sensation
Uniting the opposing and resisting forces
In lascivious revelation

Relaxation
Negation of myself as a unit
    Vacuum interlude
I should have been emptied of life
Giving life[1]

When this child, Oda Janet, died from meningitis two days after her first birthday, Mina stayed up all night and made her sculpture *The Wooden Madonna*, which is dark in every sense. There can scarcely be any more terrible lines than those which tell of the male running upstairs to his mistress while his wife lies beneath the upper floor in agony, surpassing the pain and herself. Nothing speaks louder of the anguish than that gap in the

Mina Loy, *Fashion Designs*, c. 1914, watercolour.

Mina Loy, *Surreal Scene*, 1930, collage and gouache.

text between the mountain of the belly and its goading – what a word – and the unavoidable. We sense there is absolutely no way out of the traversal of one's own female ego into its negation and the terribleness of the lines: 'I should have been emptied of life/Giving life.' She was not, but the result did nothing to decrease the anguish. It all seemed not worth it, the least one can say. *The Wooden Madonna* speaks loudly of that, as does the poem 'Ada Gives Birth to Ova', a subsection of *Anglo-Mongrels and the Rose*:

> Her face
> screwed   to the mimic-salacious
> grotesquerie of a pain
> larger than her intellect
>   They pull
> A clotty bulk of bifurcate fat
> out of her loins
> to lie
> for a period   while   performing hands
> pour lactoid liquids through
> and then mop up   beneath it
> their golden residue
>   . . .
> The soul
> apprenticed to the butcher business
> offers organic wares
> to sensibility
> A dim inheritor
> Of this undeniable flesh[2]

Stanley Cavell speaks of this poem in terms of ecstasy, saying that 'Loy's "Parturition" is a poem haunted by ecstatic data.' 'I am self-conscious ego.' Here he quotes Emily Dickinson:

Pain – has an Element of Blank –
It cannot recollect
When it begun – or if there were
A time when it was not –

He refers us, for this poem and its 'centre', to Ralph Waldo Emerson's 'Circles' and to cheerfulness in Nietzsche's *Ecce homo*. 'Maybe I have here succeeded in expressing this contrast [between the starry and the saint] in a cheerful and at the same time

Mina Loy in Paris, *c.* 1906, photograph by Stephen Haweis.

sympathetic manner — maybe that is the only purpose of the present work.'³

Any irony here is, as often, mixed with excruciating pain. She was always to excel in the satiric, the witty putdown of the world she inhabited. In her dress, in her appearance, she excelled; her marriage, whose appearance she had to maintain in order to receive her father's financing, was less successful. She became the lover of the wonderfully named Dr Henri Joël Le Savoureux, who had treated her neurasthenia after Oda's death, but was obliged to marry someone his parents had chosen. Pregnant from their relationship, she despaired still more, plagued by guilt and self-pity. At the centre of the equally well-titled poem 'Café du Néant' (not published until 1914), there is the pain not of labour, but of deep melancholy, as the woman smiles bravely in the nothingness of the couple's future and the grey winter of Paris.

To Stephen she offered half her income if they could divorce and keep it from her father, for she would have to forfeit her father's payments in the case of divorce. He refused and they then moved to Florence, Mina pregnant and unhappy amid the tea-drinking formalities of the Anglo-Florentine community and their residence outside the city itself. It seemed a museum devoted to its past. 'I would rather be a work of art than own one,' Oscar Wilde is said to have said, and, despite Mina's constant self-doubt, she dressed as a work of art. She could do that, in a major mode, given her extraordinary looks.

Vernon Lee, under the name of Violet Paget, the author of many works on psychological aesthetics as well as supernatural fiction, invited Stephen to the group gathered around her.

Mina Loy in Florence, c. 1909, photograph by Stephen Haweis.

Among them was Gordon Craig, who enlisted Stephen to make illustrations for a theatre with moveable screens, unlike traditional stage sets. Stephen also made some drypoints and plates for Craig's magazine, *The Mask*. He mixed with the Papini group at the lending library Gabinetto Vieusseux, which was within

Mina Loy and Joella, 1907.

walking distance from the Costa San Giorgio where he and Mina resided. Stephen recounted that his leaving Italy for Paris must have resulted from his quest for the 'strange and exaggerated vices in the depraved French capital'.[4]

Mina would present Isadora Duncan as the representative of the modern woman, for her free spirit. In Florence Stephen and Mina would sometimes visit the Caffè Giubbe Rosse (the opposite of the 'Café du Néant'), where artists gathered, including Giovanni Papini, with whom Mina would become involved after the difficulties of her pregnancy.

Stephen acknowledged the girl born from Mina and Henri Joël's relationship as 'Joella Synara' – as in Ernest Dowson's well-known poetic line: 'I have been faithful to thee, Cynara, in my fashion.' Soon, in 1909, Mina gave birth to Giles, her son with Stephen, who took him away to the Caribbean: Giles later died of cancer at the age of fourteen. Meanwhile, Joella's legs were not developing properly. Mina turned to a Christian Science practitioner, and from then on followed the religion and its teachings. As Joella described them later:

> My mother, tall, willowy, extraordinarily beautiful, very talented, undisciplined, a free spirit with the beginning of too strong an ego; my father, short, dark, a mediocre painter, bad tempered, with charming social manners and endless conversation about the importance of his family.[5]

So Stephen – whose paintings were selling, and whose mistress, Amelia Defries (clever in her praise, for, she said, Napoleon and Beethoven had been short men), longed to marry him – decided to take himself off to Australia. There, he avowed, he would practise meditation and sexual abstinence. Stephen rather indulged in flowery cadences, not like those of his preacher father but with the same kind of eloquence: 'Towns and great cities are like cells of energy in a mighty brain which is now slowly awakening to a newer consciousness.'[6] His studio was rented, happily, to the young Frances Simpson Stevens. Frances was a Christian Scientist, reaffirming Mina Loy in that faith, and at this point in her life Mina Loy turned from art to poetry. By 1912 she was enjoying the company and the grand parties of Muriel Draper, the lover of the pianist Arthur Rubenstein, who was even more of a vivid hostess in the cultural sense than Mabel Dodge.

And Isadora

There she encountered all sorts of highly visible artists and personalities, including the set designer Gordon Craig, with wildly flowing hair and velveteen garments, whom Stephen had already met, and who was seized up in his glamorous and spectacular affair with the barefoot dancer Isadora Duncan. Mina's poem in honour of Isadora, brief but flowing, seems just right for the grandness and openness of the multitalented Isadora's character, quite closely resembling what the free-flowing dancer would most likely have wanted. An entirely appropriate original melody is instantly recognizable.

> Songge Byrd
> for Isadora Duncan
>
> Gossip-blown songstress
> you flew upon men

>   caressed them
>   with the feathers of your eyes
>   seeing without the censor of surprise
>   that like yourself
>   descended from the skies
>   so many gods.⁷

How wonderful to be blown by the breath of gossip, which seems just right for the free-flowing or flying dance with unconstrained garments which never hemmed in Isadora. The very lightness of her dance, feathery, is attributed to her glance, heavenly in its descent and multiple, a pagan caress just blown in. Mina Loy's own elegant costuming, so often remarked upon, bears some light relation to that of this songstress (minus the 'stress'). As Roger Conover points out in the notes to this unpublished document in *The Last Lunar Baedeker*, 'These lines occur in "Biography of Songge Byrd", an unfinished verse biography of Isadora Duncan.'⁸

In 1913 there occurred the all-time important second Post-Impressionism exhibition, put on by the wide-ranging and infinitely charming Roger Fry, whose wife was forever doomed to an asylum and whose beloved Vanessa Bell had fallen irremediably in love with the brilliant and gay Duncan Grant. They were all there: the Europeans Bonnard, Matisse, Picasso and Cézanne, along with Vanessa and Duncan, Stanley Spencer and Wyndham Lewis, whom Mina Loy (who had known him before, in Montparnasse) particularly appreciated. With Frances, Mina was swept up in the world of the Futurists, of Marinetti and Papini, and of Vitalism, which would be of crucial importance to her from now on.

Filippo Tommaso Marinetti, *c.* 1916, postcard of photograph by G. Caminada, G. Ballerini & C. Editori, Florence.

INTERVAL: FUTURISM

During her time in Florence, Mina Loy was closely involved with Futurism through her amorous affairs with first Filippo Tommaso Marinetti and then Giovanni Papini, who were not exactly enchanted with each other. Each was related to a group of Futurists: Marinetti from his rather grand home in Milan, and his journal, *Poesia*; Papini to the Florentine Futurists and his journals – *La Voce* and then, appearing on 1 January 1913, *Lacerba*. Their personalities were entirely different, and that difference is one of the more fascinating elements of the way in which Futurism and its followers and dislikers developed over time.

Marinetti

The personality of Marinetti had much to do with his writing style – and his declaiming style – in the manifestos of Futurism. Here is a thumbnail of his being as it appeared. As R. W. Flint described him, at the time when Gabriele D'Annunzio self-exiled in France, Marinetti became the 'master of the revels in Italy[. He was] Very rich, personable, loyal and courtly toward friends, immensely energetic, a maniac for action and overtness at any cost." This goes a long way to explaining his attraction for Mina Loy and for an immense public, who accorded him ovations at every appearance. Born in Alexandria and taught in French by Jesuits, it is not without interest that he began his career by reciting French poetry on stages in France and Italy. Sprung, as it were, from the loins of D'Annunzio – 'the famous entertainer, master plagiarist of Decadence, high priest of Passatismo, sportsman, pilot, synthetic English country gentleman' – Marinetti made his way over Europe.[2] In London he recited his 'Battle of Adrianople' with 'machine-gun noises, cannon noises, whinnies and yells, at the top of one of the most powerful sets of lungs in Europe'. Wyndham Lewis reported that even at the Front, 'when bullets whistled around him, he had never encountered such a terrifying volume of noise.'[3]

He used a megaphone, as no one but P. T. Barnum had done before him in Europe, and was 'the first wholesale Italian enthusiastic for American promotional techniques, the first important Italian disciple of Whitman and yawper of the barbaric yawp', as when he blew his silver trumpet from the loggia of the Clock Tower in Venice and hurled down thousands of Futurist leaflets.[4] 'Aesthetic Futurism in its earliest years was far more vital and influential, interesting and exhilarating, than the Mussolinian aesthetics that cause only laughter and dismay in much of the rest of the world.' This was, says Flint, 'not even tragic, pathetic is the better word.' Flint also relates the reflection of Walter Benjamin on Marinetti admitting

> that Fascism expects war to supply the artistic gratification of a sense of perception that has been changed by technology. This is evidently the consummation of *'l'art pour l'art.'* Mankind, which in Homer's time was an object of

contemplation for the Olympian gods, now is one for itself. Its self-alienation has reached such a point that it can experience its own destruction as an aesthetic pleasure of the first order. This is the situation of politics which Fascism is rendering aesthetic.[5]

In his lauding of his own manifestos, Marinetti contrasts his innovation with his view of the outdated Victorian style of Stéphane Mallarmé:

This new array of type, this variety of colours, this original use of characters enable me to increase many times the expressive power of words. By this practice I combat the decorative and 'precious' style of Mallarmé that cause only laughter and dismay in much of the rest of the world, his recherché

Giovanni Papini, 1913, photograph by Mario Nunes Vais.

language. I also combat Mallarmé's static ideal. My reformed typesetting allows me to treat words like torpedoes and to hurl them forth at all speeds: at the velocity of stars, clouds, aeroplanes, trains, waves, explosives, molecules, atoms.[6]

For Mina, Marinetti and his enormous energy – that kind of Vitalism he embodied and communicated to her – were essential, and, as she worried about the war, she still felt herself to be young. As Italy was preparing to enter the First World War, Marinetti volunteered in a cyclist unit and Mina as a nurse in a Red Cross hospital, writing to Carl Van Vechten, 'I've got the war fever so badly . . . My masculine side longs for war.' To Mabel Dodge, she wrote later that Marinetti had assured her that she was an exception to his contempt for women, and added that although 'FTM's interest in me lasted only two months of war fever . . . I am indebted to FTM for twenty years added to my life from mere contact with his exuberant personality.'[7]

Mina was always to feel that

the vitality I learned from Marinetti . . . has not abated. That inimitable explosive – rejuvenates his familiars, though I think I have reacted to it – exactly the way I have noticed men do – Of course being the most female thing extant – I'm somewhat masculine. Do you know, I shall be quite upset if anything happens to either of those men . . . I am approaching the predicted fruition of my life. I've learnt how to be happy enough to live.[8]

Both Futurist lovers appreciated her writings. 'Marinetti said I'm a big genius,' she wrote to Carl Van Vechten, '& Papini has read some of my stuff – & says delightful things when he's not in a bad temper.' She had read Marinetti parts of the Futurist dialogue in 'The Sacred Prostitute', in which she debates him on the woman question.[9] However, she was tiring of Florence, feeling more American than English, and found it a 'stagnant hole'. She felt grateful to the Futurists for her own vivifying, but needed to get on with her life away from Florence.

Giovanni Papini

We might start with Marinetti's view of his rival, who, after *La Voce*, founded *Lacerba* in 1912, and who by the end of 1913 had rebelled, bolted from Futurism, taking Ardengo Soffici with him.

Marinetti says, not very kindly:

> as for Papini, he has neither the physique nor the voice for the part. Very myopic, with a thin monotonous voice, he reads his speech against passeist Rome badly, which I then hurl from the footlights in fistfuls of manifestos . . . I violently throw in your faces the speech of my great friend, the antiphilosophical Futurist, Giovanni Papini![10]

Obsessed with Marinetti, who was much more successful and better-looking than him – an obsession that emerged in all his relations with Mina – Papini certainly turned out differently from Marinetti. He converted to Catholicism in 1930 as 'the great penitent' and spoke of a fascist Dante. He wrote a life of Christ and grew progressively more conservative. *Lacerba* disappeared in 1914, and Papini blasted: 'Gifted Italians, like the damned in Dante always look backward . . . I found I had joined a church

Futurists and *Vociani* in Florence in 1914.
From left to right: Palazzeschi, Carrà, Papini, Boccioni and Marinetti.

Interval: Futurism 43

or academy or sect more attractive and picturesque than many others, but one in which faith was valued over freedom, noise over creation, reputation over discovery, submission to gospel over richness of experiment.'[11]

One of the most revealing events between the warring factions was an incident many times recounted as a true punch-up. One evening in 1913 Carlo Carrà arrived at the Futurist headquarters in Milan with a copy of *La Voce* that attacked a recent Futurism exhibit by Ardengo Soffici, who was exhibiting in Florence. Consequently, the Milan Futurists took the train to Florence and found Soffici in the Caffè Giubbe Rosse. Umberto Boccioni slapped him, and so on, and then the Milanese took the train back to Milan. This was yet another Futurist evening, which were generally exciting to all. Luigi Russolo would perform with his noisemakers: 'howlers, roarers, cracklers, whistler, rubbers, buzzers, exploders, gurglers, and rustlers'.[12] Description of any of the evenings or of Marinetti feel cumulative: one sees him pawing the ground, dust rising all over, swearing and attacking, and in his manifestos themselves one hears the note of alarm. This is often pointed out as a true portent of the European war about to take place.

All very Futurist. F. W. Flint maintains, and it makes a great deal of sense to me, that Alfred Jarry was the strongest influence on Marinetti, with his adoration of cars, the cult of automobilism, the delivery as depicted by André Gide of Jarry 'got up like a circus clown and acting a strenuously contrived role which showed no human characteristics . . . his bizarre unplacable accent – no inflection or nuance and equal stress on every syllable, even the silent ones'.[13] Jarry, a friend of Marinetti, published in his *Poesia* – everything feels intertwined.

The Manifestos

Herewith a gathering of some of the manifestos: for how could any reflection about Futurism exist without this kind of public manifest excitement, launched by Marinetti in 1909 (the romanticized beginning of the first manifesto: 'we had stayed up all night') and 1914, when war took over and Marinetti was otherwise engaged?

F. T. Marinetti

The Founding and Manifesto of Futurism (in *Le Figaro*, 20 February 1909), trans. R. W. Flint)

> We had stayed up all night, my friends and I, under hanging mosque lamps with domes of filigreed brass, domes starred like our spirits, shining like them with the prisoned radiance of electric hearts. For hours we had trampled our atavistic ennui into rich oriental rugs, arguing up to the last confines of logic and blackening many reams of paper with our frenzied scribbling.
>   An immense pride was buoying us up, because we felt ourselves alone at that hour, alone, awake, and on our feet, like proud beacons or feeding the hellish fires of great ships, alone with the black spectres who grope in the redhot bellies of locomotives launched down their crazy courses, alone with drunkards reeling like wounded birds along the city walls.[14]
>
> What a stage set of excitement and gilded with shining metal, stars above inside and out, richness and excess,

solitary geniuses, in a blaze of transcription. This is
surely the beginning of a poetic movement deliberately
couched in a fictional baroque romanticism.

It is from Italy that we launch through the world this violently
upsetting incendiary manifesto of ours. With it, today, we,
establish *Futurism* . . . For too long has Italy been a dealer in
second-hand clothes. We mean to free her from the number-
less museums that cover her like so many graveyards.

Museums: cemeteries!
. . .
So let them come, the gay incendiaries with charred fingers!
Here they are! Here they are! . . . come on! set fire to the
library shelves! Turn aside the canals to flood the museums!
. . . Oh, the joy of seeing the glorious old canvases bobbing
adrift on those waters, discoloured and shredded! . . . Take
up your pickaxes, your axes and hammers and wreck, wreck
the venerable cities, pitilessly![15]

And from Valentine de Saint-Point's *Futurist Manifesto of Lust*
of 1913 (published as a leaflet by the Direzione del Movimento
Futurista, Milan, 12 January 1913):

Lust, when viewed without moral preconceptions and as an
essential part of life's dynamism, is a force.
Lust is the expression of a being projected beyond itself.[16]

And Marinetti's major stylistic statement, called the *Destruction of
Syntax – Imagination without Strings – Words-in-Freedom* of 1913:[17]

The earth shrunk by speed. New sense of the world, to be
precise: One after the other, man will gain the sense of his
home, of the quarter where he lives, of his region, and finally
of the continent. Today he is aware of the whole world.

. . . a loathing of curved lines, spirals, and the tourniquet.
Love for the straight line and the tunnel . . . Dread of slow-
ness, pettiness, analysis, and detailed explanations. Love of
speed, abbreviations, and the summary. 'Quick, give me the
whole thing in two words!'

Casting aside every stupid formula and all the confused
verbalisms of the professors, I now declare that lyricism is
the exquisite faculty of intoxicating oneself with life, of filling
life with the inebriation of oneself. The faculty of changing
into wine the muddy water of the life that swirls and engulfs
us. The ability to colour the world with the unique colours of
our changeable selves.

I mean the absolute freedom of images or analogies,
expressed with unhampered words and with no connecting
strings of syntax and with no punctuation.

The imagination without strings, and words-in-freedom, will
bring us to the essence of material . . . Instead of humanizing
animals, vegetables, and minerals (an outmoded *style*, making
it live the life of material. For example, to represent the life of
a blade of grass, I say, 'Tomorrow I'll be greener."[18]

It is not that these models hold out a programme which
could stretch far beyond themselves, but we might salute this

enthusiasm as a contagious good, as the ideas and styles of Futurism at its best.

Futurism and Cubo-Futurism

Umbro Apollonio, in his edition of the Futurist manifestos, has described the differences between Cubism and Futurism. As he points out, the Cubists took advantage of polyocular vision, 'so that the object is in a static situation, involved in relations with other objects and the environment, whereas the futurists, for the most part, superimposed one object on another, or the environment on the object'.[19] The Futurists, he states, did not understand the Cubist sense of dynamic tension.

Flint sees Futurism as the forerunner of Dada, 'a flagrant imitation', claiming that the French never invented anything, but had a 'matchless talent for keeping attention on themselves'.[20] He points out further that among the fomenters of modernism – Picasso, Apollinaire, Marinetti – not one was French. It is not without interest to imagine Flint and the Italians as opposed to all the Francophiles; not very unlike how Marinetti and the Milan Futurists were opposed to Florence and the Florentine Futurists. Regional oppositions make the intensity of claims all the more appealing for both sides. The fact that Apollinaire's 'L'anti-tradition futuriste' was first published in Italian, in *Lacerba*, lends at least some irony to the situation.

In her *Futurism*, Jane Rye stresses the importance for describing the Futurist 'states of mind' (as in the so-titled Boccioni paintings of 1911) of Henri Bergson's *Matter and Memory* of 1910, in which he says that 'There is no perception which is not full of memories. With the immediate and present data of our senses we mingle a thousand details out of our past experience . . . Does not the fiction of an isolated object imply a kind of absurdity, since this object borrows its physical properties from the relations which it maintains with all others[?].'[21] As everything illuminates everything else, many of the reachings out of the Futurists reach into our interest in Mina Loy's life, loves and work. Her lifelong dealing with design – such as her lampshades and lighted globes – led her to advocate the anti-neutralist clothing sponsored by Marinetti and Francesco Cangiullo: 'it should include no neutral colors and possess the Futurist characteristic of flexibility and lack of symmetry as well as phosphorescence and perishability.'[22]

Futurism's influence upon poetics and poems outside of Italy has been stressed, for example, in Soffici's *Fine di un Mondo* (End of a World) from 1955, which sees Futurism as a 'strange mixture of D'Annunzianism, Victor-Hugoism, and Americanism'.[23] Surely, Hart Crane and his devotion to Whitman betray a Marinettian stance. Take, for example, Crane's *The Bridge* of 1930:

> Stars prick the eyes with sharp ammoniac proverbs
>   . . . but fast in whirling armatures,
> As bright as frogs' eyes, giggling in the girth
> Of steely gizzards – axle-bound, confined
> In coiled precision, bunched in mutual glee
> The bearings glint, – O murmurless and shined
> In oilrinsed circles of blind ecstasy![24]

Among the many reasons to bring Crane into Mina Loy's story is the style and more – look at this poem, so like hers in its hard-edged sight and precise sensations (these sharp ammoniac proverbs), the mechanical intrusions and speedy Futurist inclined pace (this coiled precision, these whirling armatures), the combined words (murmurless, oilrinsed), the architectural and animal (steely gizzards) – and then there is the overwhelming thought of Crane's loss and probable suicide in the Gulf of Mexico and Cravan's loss somewhere near or in that watery grave . . .

In the *Lost Lunar Baedeker: Poems*, Roger Conover says that 'Three Moments in Paris' 'is the first of a series of poetic satires on gendered roles and male/female relations'. Here, Mina Loy warms up her satiric voice to address some of the themes she explored during and immediately after the years she spent in Florence – male posturing, female dependency, marital appearance, sexual repression, romantic love. Here, too, she appropriates Futurist vocabulary in mocking defiance of Futurism's founding impresario and chief ideologue, to whom 'One O'Clock at Night' is addressed.[25]

Mina Loy never fails to surprise us. Who would have predicted the affair with Marinetti or many other things about her? From my point of view, she was always involved with significant and bizarre persons, like the superweird Oelze, the failed artist around whom the novel *Insel* revolves, or, of course, her major involvement with Arthur Cravan, the immensely tall and immensely noticeable poet and boxer and much else. Or then, her perhaps astonishing fidelity to Christian Science and thus her intimacy with Joseph Cornell, a Science faithful.

Here is the bizarre and over-the-top beginning of 'One O'Clock at Night':

> Though you had never possessed me
> I had belonged to you since the beginning of time
> And sleepily I sat on your chair beside me

> Leaning against your shoulder
> And your careless arm across my bac   gesticulated
> As your indisputable male voice   roared
> Through my brain and my body
> . . .
> Beautiful half-hour of being a mere woman
> The animal woman
> Understanding nothing of man
> . . .
> Anyhow who am I that I should criticize your theories of
>   plastic velocity
>
> 'Let us go home   she is tired   and wants to go to
>   bed.'[26]

'One O'Clock at Night' is addressed to Marinetti, the flamboyant (and inventive) founder of Futurism – a highly visual poetic language, with its emphasis on the verb for its energy and its elimination of punctuation – whose *Futurist Manifesto* was composed, as we saw him portraying, as if it were a collective gesture, a melodramatic night scene surrounded by gloriously coloured tapestries.

And then, in another voice, as if in a ventriloquist performance, she announces within quotation marks, as if the voice were to be that of Marinetti alluding to the weakness inherent in her femaleness: 'Let us go home   she is tired   and wants to go to bed.' The gaps between the words 'back' and 'gesticulated' and 'male voice' and 'roared' and then between 'Anyhow' and 'who am I' seem to make it still more a performance of the sleepy and giving-in woman and the strong male. Then the final line becomes yet more performance-like: she says it, uses the third person, and

Interval: Futurism

retires. All of this is rather astonishing in its argument about possession and non-possession, male voice and female-responding male voice, when she ceases her femaleness, to say nothing about the physical gesturing of giving up and then not giving up.

Speaking of surprise, we are not surprised that this poem is eliminated from a later collection. The whole question of performance and self-performance comes up throughout Mina Loy's life, and is certainly one of the more fascinating issues of writing a 'biography' or 'critical life' of such a multi-personed personality, an issue referred to in the Introduction, likening her multitudes within and without herself to Fernando Pessoa.

In this telescoping of place, the 'Café du Néant' has every feeling of being French – in fact, Parisian – but with life and light shouldering death, all on a diagonal. This makes it all the more black-and-white *film noir* in its extraordinarily café-anywhere feeling – but of course, the Café of Nothing says quite a lot about where it actually is not:

> Little tapers lighted   leaning diagonally
> Stuck in coffin tables of the Café du Néant
> Leaning to the breath of baited bodies
> Like young poplars fringing the Loire
> Eyes that are full of love
> And eyes that are full of kohl
> Projecting light across the fulsome ambiente
> Trailing the rest of the animal behind them
> Telling of tales without words
> And lies of no consequence
> One way or another
> . . .

In this factitious chamber of   DEATH
The woman
As usual
Is smiling as   bravely
As it is given to her to be   brave
While the brandy cherries
In winking glasses
Are decomposing
Harmoniously
With the flesh of spectators
And at a given spot

There is one

Having the concentric lighting focused precisely upon her
Prophetically blossoms in perfect putrefaction
Yet   there are cabs outside the door.[27]

This is one extraordinary poem, with, again, its gaps between the words, as in 'One O'Clock at Night', its light and darkness, metaphorically illuminating whatever universe we are reading this in. Those little tapers and the black-garbed consumers, with their real eyes and the artificial cosmetics adorning them, and the tall tales silent and yet not telling the truth even that way are filling the mortuary chamber. How life and café tables mimic the real thing, those glasses themselves filled with the brandy cherries held in decomposing hands, but the shone-upon central character of herself now totally female, labelled as 'her', is both blossoming and putrefying even as she is awaited by possibilities of transportation outside the death chamber.

Interval: Futurism

So strangely is this poem relevant to Mina Loy's entire life, not just in Florence and her involvements with Marinetti and then Papini, that it feels less like a satire than a true-ish portrait. Another testimony to her fascination with Marinetti is the 'Sketch of a Man on a Platform':

> Man of absolute physical equilibrium
> You stand so straight on your legs
> Every plank or clod you plant your feet on
> Becomes roots for those limbs
> ...
>
> Your genius
> So much less in your brain
>
> Than in your body
> Reinforcing the hitherto negligible
> Qualities
> Of life
> That it is equally happy expressing itself
> Through the activity of pushing
> THINGS
> In the opposite direction
> To that which they are lethargically willing to go
> . . .
> Fundamentally unreliable
> You leave others their initial strength
> Concentrating
> On stretching the theoretic elastic of your conceptions
> Till the extent is adequate

> To the hooking on
> Of any – or all
> Forms of creative idiosyncracy
> While the occasional snap
> Of actual production
> Stings the face of the public.[28]

The term 'absolute' for his equilibrium just about says it all, during her period of deepest attraction to this deeply energetic and in-himself-powerful ruler and founder of Futurism. How should he be reliable? – what a drastically bourgeois word, anathema to his personality. Of course his conceptions are adequate, and of course his in-your-face-ness is stinging. The 'snap' is essential and is his energy coming across, striking us even through the lines, and the 'actual' production is as actual, in the sense of nowness, as it is performative. It is the performativeness of the poem that gets Marinetti and Futurism through to us, the readers.

More powerful poems around this topic and these larger-than-life figures abound. We know that during the summers, hot as blazes in Florence, Mina left Costa San Giorgio and sometimes went, as she did in the summer of 1914, to Vallombrosa, with Carl Van Vechten and Mabel Dodge. The three poems 'Giovanni Franchi' of 1915, written in Forte dei Marmi, Italy, about Giovanni Papini, 'Lions' Jaws', and the very funny story also of 1915, 'The Effectual Marriage; or, The Insipid Narrative of Gina and Miovanni', are personifications of Futurists. Marinetti was the disciple of Gabriele D'Annunzio, who had left Italy in 1909. They and Giovanni Papini were the three powerful members of the Futurist or 'Flabbergast' fraternity, and recur in several of Mina's poems.

Mabel Dodge in lotus position, Arcetri, c. 1913.

Papini is wonderfully described in his details: among Mina Loy's large and surprisingly different poetic talents is that of the small and telling thing. For example, about his smallest gestures:

> Giovanni Franchi's wrists flicked
> Flickeringly as he flacked them
> His wrists explained things

And the character of Gabriele D'Annunzio, his elder and mentor:

> He listened at the elder's lips
> That taught him of earthquakes and
> Of women –
> His manners were abominable
> He would kill a woman
> Quite inconspiciously it is true
> And neglect to attend her funeral
> I mean the older man
> And what he taught
> Giovanni Franchi

In this poem, as elsewhere, we learn of Mina Loy's own lessons for herself, for the point

> Was to be faithful to a man   first
> The second   to be loyal to herself first[29]

This might change as her life went on, the loyalty to herself being, as time went on, combined with a magnanimous compassion for the other, and those who would be included in the 'Compensations of Poverty' later.

Thinking of that 'loyalty to herself', we see how she writes satires of the Futurist attitude towards women, which makes her physical and emotional attraction to first Marinetti and then Papini all the more entrancing. She herself is also always captivating, not only for the persons surrounding her as they come and go and she comes and is about to go, but for her biographers. So she writes not just *The Pamperers*, about all kinds of sophisticated conversations in salons and elsewhere, but also the play *The Sacred Prostitute*, begun in 1913 and continuing to mock Futurism's attitudes and talk. In 1916 she read from it and performed it and other anti-Futurist acts in Florence, even as she was trying to make money from all sorts of commercial art (magazine covers, theatre sets, dress designs, lampshades) in order to earn enough to leave for New York: 'have only one idea in my mind – *make money* – I can turn my hand to anything that comes along and do it quickly.'[30]

'Lions' Jaws', published in the September–December 1920 issue of the *Little Review*, is what appears to be her 'final verse verdict' on her involvement with the Futurists, says Conover. It was solicited by Ezra Pound, who always greatly admired her use of language in her poetry. The identities are rather clear: D'Annunzio is Danriel Gabrunzio, Marinetti is Raminetti or Rap, and Papini is GP or Bap. She actually wrote this poem after her Florentine period, already in New York and reflecting on her Futurist adventure. This presents, as Conover points out,[31] D'Annunzio's 'insatiable lust for military and sexual trophies' and Papini's feeling of inferiority, above all to the larger-than-life Marinetti. About it, she writes to Van Vechten, 'Now dear Carlo

– If you like you can say that Marinetti influenced me – merely by waking me up – I am in no way *considered* a Futurist by futurists – & as for Papini he has in no way influenced –- *my work!* So don't say a word about it – he's very passatist – really.'[32]

Herewith some parts of 'Lions' Jaws', illustrating the characters in a splendid satiric mode, beginning with the totally preposterous D'Annunzio in his over-luxurious living manner. Witness the flower-filled bath and the several royal conquests:

1.
Far away on the Benign Peninsular
that automatic fancier of lyrical birds
Danriel Gabrunzio
with melodious magnolia
perfumes his mise en scène
where impotent neurotics
wince at the dusk

The national archangel
loved several countesses
in a bath full of tuberoses

. . .

2.
. . .
Raminetti
cracked the whip of the circus-master
astride a prismatic locomotive
ramping the tottering platform

of the Arts
of which this conjuring commercial traveler
imported some novelties from
Paris in his pocket –
souvenirs for his disciples
to flaunt
at this dynamic carnival

The erudite Bapini
experimenting in auto-hypnotic Godhead
on a mountain
rolls off as Raminetti's plastic velocity
explodes his crust
of library dust
. . .
While Flabbergastism boils over
and RAM and BAP
each other's sounds
this Duplex-Conquest
claims a 'sort of success'
for the Gabrunzio resisters

3. *Envoy*
. . .
Riding the sunset
DANRIEL GABRUNZIO
corrects the lewd precocity
of Raminetti and Bapini
with his sonorous violation of Fiume

and drops his eye
into the fatal lap
of Italy[33]

The short stature of D'Annunzio (he was 5 foot 5 inches tall, 166 cm) in no way halted his amorous adventures and his long affair with the great actress Eleonora Duse. His arrogance, making himself the head of Fiume, among other elements of this soldier, playwright, administrator and just about everything else, made him a perfect icon of the so flagrantly famous male, conquering all, violating much and riding over the scholastic temperament of Papini and the flaming and drastic theatricality of Marinetti, like a hero riding into the sunset.

All this was perceived by Mina with her acute and satirically brilliant eye and pen. Her humour gets straight across, as in 'The Effectual Marriage; or, The Insipid Narrative of Gina and Miovanni', in their arrogance perfectly mirrored in the gaps between the terms, like so many mocking mirrors, with the domineering Marinetti clearly portrayed:

Gina and Miovanni   who they were God knows
They knew   it was important to them

This being of who they were
They were themselves
Corporeally   transcendentally   consecutively
conjunctively   and they were quite   complete
. . .
Ding dong   said the bell
Miovanni   Gina called

> Would it be fitting for you to tell
> the time for supper
> Pooh   said Miovanni   I am
> Outside time and space
>
> Patience said Gina   is an attribute
> And she learned   at any hour to offer
> The dish   appropriately delectable[34]

Now, it must be admitted that much of it is just that, delectable.

'Prototype', which Mina wrote in 1914, starkly contrasts religious ritual and ideal with what actually occurs in the poverty of the world outside a religious monument.[35]

> In the Duomo, on Xmas Eve, midnight
> a cold wax baby is born – born of the
> light of 1,000 candles.
> He is quite perfect, of that perfection
> which means immunity from
> the inconsistencies of Life.
>
> Perfect in pink-&-whiteness, in blue-
> eyedness, in yellow-silk-curledness
> & nearly as bright as the tinsel star
> that rises on his forehead.
>
> Worship him, for his infinitesimal
> mouth has no expansiveness for a puck-
> ering to the heart-saving wail of the
> new-born Hungry One.

> In the Duomo at Xmas Eve, midnight,
> there is another baby, a horrible little
> baby – made of half warm flesh;
> flesh that is covered with sores – carried
> by a half-broken mother.
>
> And I who am called heretic,
> and the only follower in Christ's foot-steps
> among this crowd adoring a wax doll
> – for I alone am worshipping the poor
> sore baby – the child of sex igno-
> rance & poverty.

Here is the Duomo, here is Mina Loy's own heartfelt protest against the heartlessness of many, in direct relation to her work in and life in and writing about New York's Bowery. Let us not lose sight of that, even as we meander through other parts of her variegated scenes and dramas of her living and being.

3

DIVERSIONS, 1914–53

Gathered, in various genres, *Stories and Essays of Mina Loy*, edited by Sara Crangle, are fragments and entire pieces, some of which were too long to be included in the other assemblages of Mina Loy's writings.[1] Of particular interest here are those that directly refer to other writings and incidents we know of in Mina Loy's life. I will try to discuss them in approximate order according to the notes in this bravely edited book.

We could begin with the short story 'Gloria Gamma', a very funny satire of the vanguard group of artists whom she encountered at Mabel Dodge's residence near Florence in 1907. In her useful Notes, which include various markings in the manuscripts held at the Beinecke Library of Yale University in New Haven, Sara Crangle says that MABEL is written in a large hand near the top of the last page, where also we see Mabel's first husband's name, Edwin Dodge, beneath the male called Antony.

The story opens with a perfect character sketch of the celebrated Mabel Dodge (whom we might associate with Taos, as Mabel Dodge Luhan, a columnist for the Hearst organization and a patroness of the arts, sponsor of the Armory Show and on and on), through whom Mina met Carl Van Vechten, so important to her and helpful to her writings, and also Gertrude Stein, on whom

Gertrude Stein in a birdbath as Buddha, Tuscany, c. 1910.

Mina wrote several times. Mabel Dodge's Villa Curonia, in the Medici style in Arcetri, near Florence, was a celebrated gathering place for the artistic community, Anglo-American and wider, who assembled in this grand villa and its perfected surroundings:

> Gloria Gammage had arrived at Palms with regulation social intentions – her palace was tremendous and stuffed

with things bought in the hurry of a woman with taste – and scattered around in the harmonious untidiness of temperament – erratically weeded in access of surfeit it was changing gradually to an ordered setting for what was most durable in her personality –

Here is something I find true of most of Mina's prose writings: they often feel long, and in general begin with descriptions that set the tone for the whole length of the writing. In this early story, about a famous hostess and philanthropist, we get the picture immediately – it does not change its course, only its plot. The excess of everything gives us the clue, as does the untidiness, for later we feel here 'whole vitality', part of that Vitalism so much a part of Mina's value system. It is associated with Henri Bergson, who is mentioned a few paragraphs later, where a certain bodily and mental excitement surges to the surface:

> She had the divine female quality of lending to every latest science or philosophy no matter how mathematical or how austere – a ribald flavour of lubriciousness – with her insidious interest – she at this time was passing around 'Bergson' to her friends – discoursing on it with those luscious eyes searching lovingly over their spiritual persons – that seemed to assure them that being was indeed as they had long suspected – an infinite orgy.[2]

Gloria is 'one of those who exhaust modes of being in bursts of emptiness', so that the excess of tasteful things, and the luxury of it all, are in war against that void. This happens frequently in

Mina's writings, in which the females are often dependent on males, and angry about it.

'Pazzarella' of 1913 is a perfect example. The impossibly clinging female, attached to the impossibly impossible male narrator – that is, Giovanni Papini, the addressee of the *Songs to Joannes* – is a self-satire by Mina of Mina, with a change of hair colour and a self-mocking tone.

> Golden-haired, seated before the tarnished gilding of a dilapidated clavichord, she let her idle fingers under their crepuscular jewels crawl over the keys, evoking tired melodies that sobbed and slipped into the silence without defining their complaint.

Here is the woman who will be entreating the male narrator to possess her, and this plea continues for the entire length of the story. She clings to him, desiring a child from him (but it cannot come to pass because of *Mafarka*, the creation of Marinetti, with whom Papini remains obsessed – jealously and otherwise – and clearly, Mina also).

What is fascinating here is the writer's lengthy self-mockery as a dying feeble female, opening the opportunity for the hysterically over-the-top male protagonist, who declares himself the opposite of 'an ordinary man, with no great intellect' and therefore powerful over her 'female soul ... After all, even if she loved me, she was still a human being' and 'I could consider her case at my leisure, impartially.' Now ensues the statement of power, easily mocked with that kind of excess of which Mina Loy is capable, no matter whom she is mocking or praising:

> In the divine manner, it was from this chaos I drew my inspiration. At once I grew enormous – omnipotent. After centuries of mystery, I had found the solution– a solution that lay in myself. The secret of woman is that she does not yet exist. Being a creator, I realized I can create woman. I decided to 'create' Pazzarella.³

So the woman is a non-entity, void of meaning and malleable to any force, including that of the female writer, in a spectacular casting of cruelty on to the male and of fragility on to the female: of both sides of herself we are well aware.

As for the strong beginnings of stories: in 'Transfiguration' of 1917, the opening line could scarcely be improved, for its hallucinating image from the train window. This refers to the train Mina Loy took from New York to join Arthur Cravan, who had written begging her to come and marry him. It certainly starts with a jolt: 'Outside the window a dead man hung from a tree beside the rack, and the wind moved in his trousers.'

Details like that one protrude from the Mina Loy text and upon their weight the story often hangs. Here two woman travellers, Mina the European and a Mexican woman, will be sharing hard-boiled eggs, and the salt to give them flavour is missing: 'In my lap, saltless, in white impotence to the appetite, lay six hard boiled eggs: the sullen light from the ceiling filmed in their slippery spheres.' The Mexican woman leads them to the Indians to beg salt, and it is the salt for these eggs that lends its full flavour to the text, as tasteful in its telling as any visual writing can be. 'I held my cupped palm before me as I walked over the rocking flints, carrying the rough and turgid crystals carefully as a sacrament through the dark where the parted forest reared over the steel ribbons of the railroad.'[4]

Among all these stories, with their odd beginnings and details, one sticks out as quite remarkable: 'The Stomach'. It is peculiarly graphic and hard-hitting from beginning to end. Starting with a truly negative portrait of an old woman – and we cannot help reflecting on Mina Loy's uncordial relations, to put it mildly, with her own mother – this all gives off a disturbingly personal ring.

> There sat the mother.
> Where the flesh should have been, there was a shawl – the wits of the aged go wool-gathering, dutiful relatives knit them into a frowsty comfort for the blinking, twitching, wheezing forgetter of many delights.
> Her blind eye floated like a decaying fish in the dregs of her lucidity. There must have been parts of her even more terrifying than those that were exposed – in 'out of use' there is ugliness.
> Delicate and decent however were the appointments of the sitting-room, the cleared and varnished tabernacle for this bundle of human garbage.

What creepiness done with what brilliance. Such a grand use of a word is 'frowsty', a perfect example of Mina's love of and work with words, indeed, her logopoeia, as Pound put it. And throughout this incredibly strong tale, every sentence is weighted with intense *spectacularity*, if I can put it like that. The daughter cossets the mother throughout, having no time for marriage, filling the room with flowers, devoting herself for her lifetime, and employing 'her leisure with the Arts'.

Virginia Cosway, clearly quite a beauty years ago, was the model for a famous statue of *La Tarantella* over a quarter of a century old, much visited by tourists. Its presiding feature is famously 'the pose inspired by the Master, the outswung allurement, the momentary momentous projection of the stomach in the *danza española*'. Virginia performs 'her Hispano-abdominal ceremony at les vernissages, the private views, auctions of the Hôtel Druout' and so is known all over Europe for the myth, according to which she has broken the heart of the great sculptor, his guiding star. Then she spends her life doing her sacred duty with her mother, who rolls 'her surviving eye on the stomach of her attendant daughter' and wheezes out the words: 'If only she would take it out of my way – even for a day. If only I could be left alone.' This brief tale ends dreadfully, in our face, as it were, when it concludes with the narrator as ourselves, or rather 'myself', close up:

> The stomach in its age was become fibrous and rigid.
> And as it proceeded towards me, I would have sworn I could see, set in the wrinkled lids of its navel – a calculating eye.[5]

The ghastliness in the sight and insight of the entire brief story in its overcoming horror shows the pen of Mina Loy at its most powerful in these years.

The plays *The Pamperers* and *The Sacred Prostitute* are both satires of the salons and gatherings Mina Loy frequented, such as those of Mabel Dodge in Florence and in Paris, and then of the Arensbergs in New York. *The Pamperers* is an unpardoning travesty of the Futurist conversation in Milan and Florence, around

Marinetti and Papini, about which Mina Loy was never certain that the writing worked. She read *The Sacred Prostitute* at Natalie Barney's salon, and it was a stunning success for its recognizable features and persons.

In *The Pamperers*, we are treated to a heading that says it all.

TAG ENDS OF OVERHEARD CONVERSATION,

and indeed both plays sound exactly like that, with Picasso and cigar ends and Dresden china, and someone swearing, 'We shall never give up wearing silk stockings.'

Just exactly the way none of it hangs together, and Mina's irony, concurred with her elegance of bearing and wearing. They have their brilliance and could be transferred to any other gatherings of those years. The *Gate Crashers of Olympus* of 1925 deals in that way with art and Picasso, referred to by Mina elsewhere as having the importance that she could scarcely overlook – and also Braque. It is all on the level of a name game, perfect for the 'artistic' parody, readable at top speed, and no less enjoyable for that:

> The somersault of society dates from the day that a small Spaniard, P. O. Casse (*cf.* French breakage), so inevitably exhibited the portrait of a wine glass, 'looking both ways at once.'

Everything deals in great wit, with Cubism mocked for its multi-perspectival innovations, with the wine glass having its portrait painted, and the game continues:

I have heard that the original wine glass was broken by Braque, i.e., cf. break. Or at least that he broke another on the same day –

However I predict that the breakage of P.O. Casse will be canonised by the dealers – for he has successively broken a greater variety of objects, and with more rapidity than his most ardent opponents (i.e. disciples) could keep up with.

Example.

P. O. Casse broke a guitar – which prophetic pattern induced an aesthetic intimation comparable to what in other areas, the French call frisson.

This disjuncted guitar has in every 'avant guard' every year, in every land re-re-re-represented the imminent intellectual revolt for one quarter of a century.

The same guitar – often seen believe me – broken at the same place – yet bearing a variety of signatures.

I cannot imagine a more successful play on Cubistic play, in all its serious and spirit-filled richness. Of course, commerce and the dealers, and the deformation of words like 'avant-garde', and the superb repetition of the 're-re-re-re' representation of itself – even the conclusion of this short take-off is perfect, with the new 'new' in quotes to make it really 'new', and ending just with an inconclusive dash: 'Art is always "new" to the uninitiate – '[6]

If we, by some peculiar chance, had not already detected her unique satiric mode, being as slow as we, often all of us readers, give ourselves the privilege to be, we might well give up here. Picasso would have loved it.

So much about Mina Loy was in two parts that her own imagining of her thoughts, ongoing and ongone, was also divided.

Take the dialogue between Mi & Lo, from 1939, like some sort of would-be Socratic structure – which feels, as many of her prose texts feel to me at least, overlong in all its parts. It begins:

I.
FORM

>   lo

Does form result from seeing uniform repeatedly? For the first man I see is formless, in that he has no recognisable form. But the second man I see is recognisable as having the same form as the first man I have seen.

>   mi

Not so. For the one half of the first man I see is the replica of the formation of the other half of the first man I see. Thus, instantaneously he takes form. The intention of his form being endorsed by its duality. Form is the union of

Und so weiter. And on and very much on. Pages and pages.
 When Mina was living in the Bowery and caring about the inhabitants, those angelic down-and-outs who inspired her emotionally moving epic poem 'Hot Cross Bum', she wrote the essay 'Universal Food Machine', with its descriptive beginning demonstrating compassion. There is no satire and no joking here in this part of her life:

> 1. Universal Food Machine
> Open radiators at regular intervals along the streets to temperate the rigors of winter creatures who seem to come from nowhere and to be going nowhere.

This is followed by two other parts, 'II. War' and 'III. Effluvia of decomposition of the Spirit', pointing out that suffering and destruction take a toll on the soul, as on the body: 'Therefore when Christ commanded us to do unto others as we would that they should do unto us, it was as a primary measure of spiritual hygiene.'[7]

Finally then come a few words (a contrast with her often verbose prose) about the dialogue between Religion and Eros (already of interest in her early thoughts about the idea of prostitution and society, and always continuing in her own thinking and writing). Here is some of that long and of course unfinished treatise Burke dates between 1948 and 1953:

> HISTORY OF RELIGION AND EROS
>
> Since intellection outgrew the aboriginal simplicities it advanced through two seemingly irreconcilable channels
> _____
>> The mystic meditation of early Asia. The Scientific *research* of a Universe to further man's 'Domination over all things' i.e., enjoyment of surprising revelations to be drawn into the open out
>>
>> . . .
>>
>> POWER: creative dynamism, consciously operative, solely constructive.

In contacting power, lies immunity to the destructive Religion's salvation.

FORCE merely a derivative of Power isolated, by limitation of intellect from its conscious motivation.

In force lies peril, destruction, fragmentation, RELIGION'S DAMNATION.

RELIGIONS'S POWER OF GOD VERSUS REALISM'S BLIND FORCE herewith man, mistaking destruction for dominion, furthers the ultimate menace to his perfectability.

. . .

Whatever transpired in the Ego-laboratory of mystic research proved so mysterious to the occidentals that finally they easily accepted it as the mystery to end all mysteries: the nothing-at-all.

Albeit to an observer from some cosmic distance the mystery would be cleared –

It is not prohibitive to man, as the complete microcosm, to train potentialities to avail himself of his resources, akin to the atomic, electronic etc. in order to transcend the restrictions of his overt senses.

. . .

who exceptionally react to vibrational stimuli beyond the standard gamut.

. . .

THE ELEMENTARY DISCOVERY
The rhythm of breath attuning the organism it aerates to the concentration of the mind upon the abstract; each inbreath wandered – – – – [8]

Wandering a bit lost among these last late and heavy fragments and satires and treatises of this poet's mind, after the ferociously witty early essays and satires, I can sum up my thoughts about her prose, in order to offer the highest praise I can imagine in real time and space and writing: Loy was a real poet.

4

NEW YORK AND THE ARENSBERG CIRCLE, 1916–18

Nineteen-sixteen, the year in which Mina Loy sailed for New York, was a great year for poetry, and for Mina's involvement in the world of publication and of reception by readers. Her poems were beginning to appear in little magazines, including her rather far-out and remarkably concrete-sensuous love poems, like the *Songs to Joannes* (that is, Papini), with its

> Pig Cupid   his rosy snout
> Rooting erotic garbage[1]

In defending the free-verse style of his magazine *Others*, in which Mina published, Alfred Kreymborg, its editor, claimed that its presentation was a revolution against the old and 'fusty' styles, now that *we* were all geared up for a new and individual 'inside yourself' expression. This aim calls upon Mina's own declamation in her 'Aphorisms of Futurism' (it's a good thing that here, we do not have to use her later preferred term 'modernism'): 'FORGET that you live in houses that you may live in yourself.' Mina's superbly outlandish writing and style and being – for this period dates before she becomes an American citizen – speak loudly for why she is now really significant to read through the double lens of Dada and Surrealism.

A telling tribute to the importance of Mina's excruciatingly outspoken verse was unleashed by the New York *Evening Sun*'s Don Marquis, whose parody of 'Otherists' reads:

> Oh, beautiful mind,
> I lost it
> In a lot of frying pans,
> And calendars and carpets
> And beer bottles
> Oh, my beautiful mind.[2]

For him, all this was 'Yurrupean', and to some extent Mina Loy represented the import from elsewhere. Gertrude Stein's writings stirred Mina's pulse, as did those of Djuna Barnes and James Joyce. Mina's free verse, unlike the compositions of Elizabeth Barrett Browning or Christina Rossetti and then T. S. Eliot and William Carlos Williams and Wallace Stevens, was a kind of sexual liberation. We have only to look at the elaborately erotic *Songs to Joannes*, occurring in the same time as Isadora Duncan's dance and the idea of Vitalism – based on Bergson's *élan vital*. Such goings-on are not unlike Marinetti's cosmic energy, and are no less in harmony with the way Gertrude Stein had defined Italians: they are 'warmly liking being living'. Her poetry is as unlike that of those around her as is the poetry of Emily Dickinson.

If the noisy, busy movement Futurism was easy to satirize in a short play, the conversation in the Arensberg salon, into which Mina Loy was introduced soon after her arrival in New York, was no less so.

The only trouble with The Public is education.

    Education is the putting of spectacles on wholesome eyes. The Public does not naturally care about these spectacles, the cause of its quarrels with art. The Public likes to be jolly; The Artist is jolly and quite irresponsible. Art is The Divine Joke, and any Public, and any Artist, can see a nice, easy simple joke, such as the sun. But only Artists can look at a greyish stickiness on smooth canvas.
. . .
So, The Public and The Artist can meet at every point except the – for The Artist – vital one, that of pure, uneducated seeing.
. . .
You might, at least, keep quiet while I am talking.[3]

    What a delicately arranged spoof it is, with the snobbery clearly in place during the chatter about The Public and The Artist, capitalized and stressed in italics, assuming that the one speaking is allied with art, as opposed to the hoi polloi who are the other. (Of course, not the Other, as in the magazine, which took on a serious oppositional stance to such titles as Serious Critics.) Mina Loy's wit is cruelly exacting, and she knows her audience to be both perceptive and, to some extent, self-mocking, since none of us really knows who is the public and who the artist. We all want to be the artist and not just the wearer of an artist's costume.

    Furthermore, the stylistic cutting of the sentence in the middle of the statement 'the – for The Artist – vital one' speaks loudly of the mannerisms of the snob. Mina Loy knew how to spoof from the inside, and that is the avant-garde thing whose idea she valued, precisely as she personifies this poetry she claims not to have owned.

The final exclamation: 'You might, at least, keep quiet while I am speaking' is a superb put-down of the gathering as well as a mirroring of the intense egotism of the Futurist dominating maleness she has just left behind in leaving Europe for America. And, as Conover puts it: 'Throughout her career, Loy camouflaged demonstrative and theatrical first persons behind inscrutable aliases. She ventriloquized. She dissembled. She canceled.'[4] (About her novel *Insel*, which I discuss later, I totally agree with her not having a clue 'as to its merit . . . I leave that to my post-mortem examination,' as she put it.[5]) This cancelling out of her own writing is certainly one of her links to Arthur Cravan in his multiple personas, investigated and deliberated and denied by all those fascinated by him.[6]

Here is a piece from the 1917 first issue, and wonderful it is indeed. 'O Marcel!', as it was titled, is a further example of her far-out wit, since Duchamp was and remains the hero (and the self-mocking hero) not just of Dada, but of any avant-garde.[7]

The appearance of this piece in the Dada magazine *The Blind Man* demonstrated how Mina Loy was surely one of the brilliant mockers. It is more Dada than the Surrealist it preceded, and indeed much about her work and being and appearance was peculiarly prescient. She used detritus early on to construct her objects, far before the Dada passion for detritus, even before Kurt Schwitters, and she never abandoned that splendid art of poverty, even when she could have done otherwise.

The Arensberg Circle

Of all the captivating circles in which Mina Loy was involved, directly after that of Mabel Lodge in Acetri, came that of Walter and Louise Arensberg at 33 West 67th Street, New York. On the high walls of the largish apartment were displayed an enormous number of contemporary works of art by artists such as Marcel Duchamp, Pablo Picasso, Henri Matisse and Georges Braque. It was said of Walter Arensberg, 38 years old, and Louise his wife, 37, that 'they collected not only art, but the artists as well.'[8] Duchamp, 27, whose *Nude Descending a Staircase* had made such a sensation at the Armory Show, was often there, playing chess. He lived in a studio that adjoined the upper level of the Arensberg apartment through a short hallway. André Raffray's portrait/painting *An Afternoon at the Arensbergs* depicts an imagined gathering of 31 artists assembled in that large living-room, with the couple Walter and Louise in the centre, Marcel Duchamp in a large armchair with a foldover back, rather like a throne, a chess set with players at the lower right, and the extraordinary Dada personality Baroness Elsa von Freytag-Loringhoven just entering the room – making as always a staggeringly unusual appearance (here in a grass skirt and a see-through blouse, holding a glass in one hand and a cigarette with rising smoke in the other). The American Futurist painter Joseph Stella appears in the left corner with a guitar, just behind Edgard Varèse at the piano, and between him and the Arensbergs is Mina Loy, seated next to a tray table with drinks and hors d'oeuvres. The imposing figure of Arthur Cravan is seated directly in front of Mina, and various other colourful figures in perfect avant-garde accord with the variegated artworks behind them mostly gaze out at us, so that we feel part of the party.

Baroness Elsa von Freytag-Loringhoven, 1920s.

André Raffray, *Chez Arensberg*, 1984, gouache on board. From left to right: Joseph Stella (guitar in hand), Beatrice Wood (seated in armchair), Edgard Varèse (at the piano), Arthur Cravan, Mina Loy, Elmer Ernest Southard, Albert Gleizes, Juliette

Roche, Louise Arensberg, Walter Arensberg, Marcel Duchamp, Francis Picabia and Henri-Pierre Roché (playing chess), Gabrielle-Buffet Picabia, John Covert (before the fireplace), Man Ray, Baroness Elsa von Freytag-Loringhoven.

A great number of them were European refugees from war zones, and the languages spoken were many. Mina spoke several, including French, German and Italian, as well as her native English. The conversations were wide ranging, full of art-world gossip, professional and personal, for insiders and outsiders, habitual frequenters, occasional drop-ins and the newly arrived. Mina Loy's play *The Pamperers* is a perfect example of the pseudo-sophisticated conversation she was so brilliant at satirizing, both at Mabel Dodge's and the Arensbergs'.

Mina was to feel at home in the Arensberg Circle, since she had already cherished Arensberg's poem 'To a Poet' because of its irreverence for God, therein called 'the great Cosmical Non-entity', and for the poet, 'like a naughty child . . . Without a wedding and a little wild'.[9] The subject of the poem is the Circle; innumerable are the many references to perfume and fashion, with 'wit and sexual innuendo'.[10] Several members of the Circle starred in poetic performances in print and during the evenings.

On Friday 26 May 1917 the now historic Blindman's Ball was held at Webster Hall on East 13th Street, New York, to celebrate the first issue of a magazine of the same name (*The Blind Man: A Magazine of Verse Art*). To announce the occasion, the American actress Beatrice Wood, one of the magazine's editors, drew a stick figure thumbing its nose at the bourgeois world for a poster advertising the ball.

Six weeks earlier, Duchamp's famous urinal, called *Fountain*, labelled as being by R. Mutt and submitted to the Independents Exhibition at the Grand Central Palace, had been rejected, although any dues-paying member of the organization was allowed to submit two works with the assurance that they would be shown. The grounds were that it was 'too crude' to be displayed, upon which ruling both Duchamp and Arensberg resigned from the organization.

The Blind Man was defending and celebrating that Fountain and its rejection, rethinking modern art. Mina Loy and several other attendees had pieces in the magazine, and she was of course one of the principal characters – she was dressed as one of her commercially successful lampshades. The Blindman's Ball was a grand occasion for several reasons, one being that Duchamp in his tipsy state climbed the flagpole hanging over the dance floor. Then Wood performed a Russian dance, and later claimed that the Italian painter Joseph Stella – painter of the Brooklyn Bridge and Chinatown, a vertical painting on glass the Arensbergs had purchased earlier – had fought to defend her honour. She found that deliciously ironic, having been amorously and recently involved with the painter Henri-Pierre Roché: the trio Stella-Wood-Roché were just about always together for movies, restaurants and conversations at the Arensbergs. Behind the scenes was transpiring a drama frequent in such circles.[11] Roché was simultaneously involved with the hostess, Louise Arensberg, for two years, until Walter discovered it and forced it to end; Roché eventually returned to France.

After the ball they all went uptown to the Arensbergs', near Central Park West. 'If you attended the Blindman's Ball and were fortunate enough to have been invited to the Arensberg apartment afterward, you would have met some of the most important and influential people in the art and poetry world of the day. If nothing else, it was the sort of party you would never forget.'[12] Famously, Duchamp's bed that evening accommodated five of the revellers, in a scene well described by Beatrice Wood:

Since it was too late to go home, Mina Loy led several of us to spend the night at Marcel's apartment. Sleepily, we threw ourselves onto his four-poster bed and closed our eyes like a collection of worn-out dolls. Mina took the bottom of the bed with Arlene [sic] Dresser against her, and Charles Demuth, the painter, lost no time in draping himself horizontally at right angles to the women, a trouser tugged up revealing a garter. Marcel, as host, took the least space and squeezed himself tight against the wall, while I tried to stretch out in the two inches left between him and the wall, an opportunity of discomfort that took me to heaven because I was so close to him. Lying practically on top of him I could hear his beating heart, and feel the coolness of his chest. Divinely happy, I never closed my eyes to sleep.[13]

The second issue of the magazine carried the initials of the three editors – Duchamp (as 'Totor'), Henri-Pierre Roché and Beatrice Wood – on its cover: PTB. That issue contained the famous sarcastic statement sometimes attributed to Duchamp but written by Wood: 'As for plumbing, that is absurd. The only works of art America has given are her plumbing and her bridges.'[14] (This is particularly delightful given the other piece of a plumbing fixture called *God*, which was equally attributed to the Baroness Elsa Freytag-Loringhoven and to Morton Schamberg the photographer.) So much for plumbing, and for the continuation of American Dada, which appellation can certainly be given to the Arensberg salon. Mina Loy was very Dada in the great sense of the word, when she felt like it, just as she was a Futurist for a limited time. When Duchamp came across her and her object assemblages, he declaimed: 'The Baroness is not a futurist, she is the future.' Heavily involved with imaging about Duchamp, the Baroness rubbed a newspaper clipping about him all over her body and recited a poem: 'Marcel, Marcel, I love you like Hell, Marcel.'

Beatrice Wood had met Duchamp earlier when visiting another member of the Arensberg circle, the composer Edgard Varèse, who was in hospital with a broken leg. Having studied and lived in France, she could speak his language. Varèse was known for incorporating street sounds into his music, as did Guillaume Apollinaire into his poems, along with overheard conversations: modernism gets celebrated early with such intrusions from the outside world, snatches of actual songs or talk into the text or image. Louise Arensberg was particularly pleased to have him play the piano for the circle gathered in her apartment. Beatrice Wood was especially welcomed when she placed a real bar of soap in the crotch of her image of a naked woman emerging from a bath, called Un peu d'eau dans du savon (A Little Water in Some Soap). She had originally meant to title it with the soap going into the water, and just paint a piece of soap, but Duchamp persuaded her to leave it and then, instead of painting the soap over the exposed crotch, to place there instead a real piece of soap. Yet again, the

Beatrice Wood, New York, 1915.

real outside intrudes famously into the piece of art. When it was exhibited, countless men placed their calling cards into the frame, hoping the brazen artist might call them. She felt obliged to go and remove the cards time after time, and finally regretted all the attention: methinks few contemporary artists would be so reticent.

Playing chess with Roché in Charles Sheeler's 1919 photograph of the Arensberg gathering (titled *Interior of the Arensberg Apartment*) is Francis Picabia. His wife Gabrielle Buffet wrote for *Camera Work*, the magazine published by Alfred Stieglitz, to explain her husband's abstract watercolours of New York, which he had exhibited with Stieglitz. This chess game was of singular importance to the players and the wider community because of the stakes: Roché's magazine, *The Blind Man*, which had had only two issues so far, was competing against Picabia's *391*, which had already appeared seven times, and the loser would cease publication. Picabia won, and *391* continued for another seven years, until 1924, while he showed more abstract paintings at the Stieglitz Gallery in 1915 and contributed a series of mechanical portraits to a folio-sized *291*, so named because of the Stieglitz Gallery's location at 291 Fifth Avenue.

Yet another important magazine connected to the same circle was *Rogue*, published by Louise Norton, a writer and translator from French, and her husband, Allen Norton. The first issue included Gertrude Stein and Wallace Stevens, Mina's poem 'Sketch of a Man on a Platform' about Marinetti without naming him, and her 'Three Moments in Paris'. It seems that Louise had delivered *Fountain* to the Independents, keeping Duchamp's name out of it, and, progressively estranged from Allen, had taken up with Edgard Varèse, marrying him in Paris in 1922.

Relatively sophisticated chit-chat flourished, represented in the so-called 'conversation pictures' of the American painter Florine Stettheimer, and those deliberately naive portraits may have had some bearing on the stylized nudes of Juliette Roche Gleizes, whose narrative entitled 'The Mineralization of Dudley Craving Mac Adam' plays with the characters of Walter Arensberg and Arthur Cravan. She was good at parodies, and at scooping up any amusing detail: so, in her *Demi-Circle*, she captures a Brevoort Hotel conversation in which someone is ceaselessly repeating 'All is well' and the refrain 'Long live anarchy,' and then a Nietzsche quote: 'The time of great wars is coming.' Indeed it was.

As it often seemed to be in various parts of Mina Loy's life, conversation was the real point. Here is Ezra Pound describing 'the dance of the intelligence' happening all over, but especially in places like Paris and New York City. Here is Robert McAlmon speaking of the brilliant conversation of Mina Loy and Jane Heap in Paris (but it could have been anywhere): 'Mina, her cerebral fantasies, Jane, her breezy, traveling salon of the world tosh which was impossible to recall later. But neither of these ladies needed to make sense. Conversation is an art with them, something entirely unrelated to a sense of reality or logic.'[15]

Edouard Archinard (Arthur Cravan), *Sculpture in a Park*, 1914, oil on canvas.

INTERVAL: ARTHUR CRAVAN

'I have twenty countries in my memory and I drag the colours of a hundred cities in my soul.'[1] Now arrives Arthur Cravan, just presented as he might perhaps have wished.[2] And so *Maintenant*, with its five issues, has arrived and taken over the text.

About Arthur Cravan, Fabian Avenarius Lloyd, almost everything should be written in capitals with exclamation points following. Sometimes he was also Edouard Archinard,[3] and sometimes others: Isaac Cravan, Dorian Hope, Sebastian Hope, B. Holland, Robert Miadique, Marie Lowitska, W. Cooper, James M. Hayes. Why not?

When he was in the boxing ring, which happened when he needed money, he would rise and announce himself as having at least 32 occupations, including poet, professor, boxer, dandy, *flâneur*, forger, critic, sailor, prospector, card sharp, lumberjack, *bricoleur*, thief, editor and chauffeur. Of course, and this is part of the Cravan excitement, we have absolutely no idea which of these qualifications were befitting, given the multiple myths around him, none of them in the slightest uninteresting. Nothing about Cravan is slight. What is unmythical has been sketched in the Introduction, and is quite simply this. Arthur Cravan and Mina Loy had tried Mexico City, with his idea for a boxing club, which did not work out, and their resources were gone: thus they needed to go somewhere else. Mina, pregnant with Fabienne, was to go by passenger ship to Buenos Aires, which she finally did. Cravan was to follow with their friends in a small yacht, which he was trying out in Salina Cruz. He may or may not have departed oceanwards. If he did, he did not return. This unresolved ending or escape contributes to a claim I would advance: Arthur Cravan, in all the ways he named and manifested himself, was the ultimate Dada, far beyond the weakened adaptation: 'Dadaism'. One of the glorious things about his one-person publication *Maintenant* is that its presentation, as if written by various pens under various names, is reminiscent of the brilliant publication of Stéphane Mallarmé's *La Dernière Mode*, over the rereading of which Mallarmé lingered many an evening.

Impractical and Impassioned

Willard Bohn, in a piece entertainingly called 'Chasing Butterflies with Arthur Cravan', presents Cravan as representing the Dada spirit ahead of Dada itself.[4] Seems quite right to me. 'Constructed around principles such as insouciance, impermanence, defiance, and revolt, his life is best seen as the ultimate Dada gesture. "Every great artist is imbued with provocation", he used to proclaim.'[5] The art collector André Level quotes a letter from Cravan, always in need of financial support and dealing in fake Picassos and others, and I quote this because of its so Cravan-like atmosphere, impossible to fully grab to any extent. But this comes close, saying just this about Brazil and what he planned to do there:

I can only reply that I will be going to see the butterflies. Perhaps it is absurd, ridiculous, impractical, but it is stronger than me, and if I have perhaps some worth as a poet, it is precisely because I have irrational passions, excessive needs; I would like to see spring in Peru, to make friends with a giraffe and when I read in the Petit Larousse that the Amazon is 6,420 kilometers long and has the largest volume in the world, it has such an effect on me that I cannot even express it in prose.[6]

My own view is that he, like Mina Loy, was not a prose character, nor did his language turn out to be prose: rather, poetry.

About *Maintenant*: that name is in English 'Now', reminiscent of the brilliant publication of Stéphane Mallarmé's *La Dernière Mode* (The Latest Fashion), which Cravan often called a sort of dream. Mallarmé would not have objected, since he often found himself *rêvant* or dreaming over this, his own creation. *Maintenant* is in fact a gender-fluid dream, and includes texts allegedly by all sorts of persons of both sexes, exercising all sorts of professions: Mme de P, Ix, Le Chef de Bouche Chez Brabant, Olympe, une Négresse, Miss Satin, Châtelaine, a Creole Lady, a Grandmother, and a Reader from Alsace.

Far from claiming for Arthur Cravan a kind of nineteenth-century delicately elegant distinctiveness and that kind of Mallarméan intellect, I am stating how both Cravan and Loy were geniuses unlike any other, and how their multiple personalities are especially enchanting to contemplate alongside each other in their intense oppositions, like some perfect boxing match in some ideal ring.

So what most know about Cravan is that he – actually either six foot or six foot four inches, about 230 pounds and measuring

Watercolour by 'Robert Miradique' (Arthur Cravan) with a note from Blaise Cendrars, 1937, saying: 'This watercolour is by Robert Miradique, one of the numerous pseudonyms of Arthur Cravan, really named Gerald Llyod [sic], I paid him 50 centimes in cash in January 1914 for it.'

19 inches around his biceps, blond, entered the ring in Barcelona on 23 April 1916, with Jack Johnson, a hefty experienced Black man – and was knocked out in the sixth round. Arthur Cravan, as he began to call himself in 1912, was, as Conover puts it, a world tramp and totally immoderate, seeking the extremes and generally finding them, a bum; thus he was completely adapted to Mina Loy's writing so frequently about bums and indeed appropriate as a criminal-angel to her crab-angel bums. He was an elegant dresser when he chose, as he often did not, wearing torn shirts and shorts with tattoos showing or then not, throwing his dirty laundry at the audience during his lecture at the New York Independents Exhibition on 19 April 1917, on that occasion described before, when, in a state of advanced intoxication, he removed shirt, waistcoat, collar and braces, and was taken away to jail.

Cravan would wear a soldier's uniform and hitchhike to neutral ground to defy the whole idea of war. Appearance and reality were both terms to be confronted. He would sign letters as his uncle Oscar Wilde, offering them to dealers and collectors, both in London and Dublin in 1922, sometimes extending these forgeries as Sebastian Hope, representing Pierre Louÿs, one of Wilde's translators into French or holding out (necessarily fake) letters by André Gide, who modelled Lafcadio in *Les Caves du Vatican* on Cravan. How could he not? Cravan was the most preposterous and altogether unlikely match for anyone, and he and Mina Loy fell madly – that is indeed the exact word – in love.

He loved his body and so did Mina. 'Genius', he said, 'is nothing more than an extraordinary manifestation of the body.'[7] He did not just lecture, as he could, on Egyptian art, among hundreds of other topics, especially the classics and modern art, but he would always perform. At a meeting of the Société des Savants, he would fire shots into the air, scarcely what the *savants* were expecting.

Unsuspected

Nothing about Cravan is what one might suspect. I was astounded by his poetry, and found it enlivening even as it had not the twists and turns of Mina Loy's poems in all their various transmogrifications. Cravan's poems are loud and adventuresome, like himself, whereas hers are more interior in their curling around themselves, it seems to me. His are right there, obvious, like his body, and it was perhaps that body that set them body-dreaming. Here are some poems, enticing and complete in themselves, whereas in Mina Loy's, you are invited or then sent elsewhere.

All those of us fascinated by Cravan must have differing ways of keeping and sharing that fascination. Mine, at this moment of writing, is the way in which number 1 of *Maintenant* opens with a whistle, a *sifflet*:

> Le rythme de l'Océan berce les transatlantiques,
> Et dans l'air où les gaz dansent tels des toupies,
> Tandis que siffle le rapide héroique qui arrive au Havre,
> S'avancent comme des ours les matelots athlétiques.
> New York! New York! Je voudrais t'habiter.
> J'y vois la science qui se marie
>   A l'industrie,
> Dans une audacieuse modernité.
>   Et dans les palais,
>   Des globes,
>   Eblouissants à la rétine,

Interval: Arthur Cravan

> *Par leurs rayons ultra-violets,*
> *Le téléphone américain*
> *Et la douceur*
> *Des ascenseurs . . .*

Whistle

Decks lulled by the rhythm of the Ocean,
While in the air gases swirl like twirling tops,
And the heroic express arrives whistling into Le Havre,
Athletic sailors approach like bears.
New York! New York! How I want to inhabit you.
There I see the marriage of science
 And industry
With bold modernity,
 And in the Palaces,
  Globes
Which dazzle the retina
With their ultra-violet rays;
 The American telephone
 And the tranquillity
  Of elevators . . .

Mina's Colossus

Cravan's many aliases and crafty fashions for this and that made him a perfect companion for Mina Loy, given to her own numerous aliases and diverse ways of making enough to live on, here and there, over and over.[8] Her recounting of her love is found nowhere else:

Those first days in Mexico we wandered ceaselessly arm
in arm. It never made any difference what we were doing
– making love or respectfully eyeing canned goods in groceries, eating our tomatoes at street corners or walking among
weeds. Somehow we had tapped the source of enchantment,
and it suffused the world. We must have anticipated the
embrace of reunion as the consolatory Absolute which no perspective of Time could augment or reduce . . .

We both wanted to 'really' marry in a rosy Mexican cathedral, spill our excessive delight in receptive aisles splashed
with the wine and gold of stained-glass windows. Of course
the money ran short of this fantasy and the mayor had to
find two witnesses. I was so convinced of the mere formality
of Mexican ceremonies that after the vows Colossus had to
nudge me. 'If you don't make any response,' he whispered
severely, 'he'll refuse to marry us.'

'I will,' I hurriedly exclaimed.

'Now I have caught you. I am at ease.'[9]

The literary journal *Maintenant*, the way many of us first knew Arthur Cravan, was published from Cravan's address at 29 rue de l'Observatoire in Paris in 1914 and sold from a vegetable cart: very literary Dada. There is so much we don't know about him, apart from the legend, and never will. We do know that he applied for a Russian passport shortly before disappearing in Mexico in 1918. Cravan had met Trotsky aboard the *Monserrat* crossing the Atlantic, and was under surveillance by the FBI in New York and the U.S. Secret Service in Mexico.[10] In October 1917 he was wearing a military uniform and posing as a soldier on furlough to avoid conscription, and in December, from Mexico City, he sent a letter

Beatrice Wood, *Mina Loy and Arthur Cravan*, 1990, coloured pencil and graphite on paper.

imploring Mina to join him and marry him in Salina Cruz, which she did. She returned to Florence to pick up her children, taking the only available berth on a passing Japanese hospital ship bound for Buenos Aires. Never did she see him again, and she mourned him all the rest of her life.

> I had first seen his portrait in an art review in which a certain sleekness of feature gave him the air of a homosexual, and this, for the time, stripped him of all mystery for me . . . 'This is a mind which would snub mine,' I surmised, as I studied the portrait. 'It deals in values of luxury.' His clothes, his surroundings, looked expensive. A couple of Siamese cats lay among his negligent hands . . .
> It was on my second meeting with him that I perceived him as beautiful . . . This second encounter took place at a party in Walter's apartment . . . among the elegant couples gathered there. He was wrapped in a sheet whose encasement gave the perfect construction of his case the significance of sculpture . . .
> Colossus, with whom I had still not spoken, slunk down beside me . . . (by this time he had taken off his sheet and towel) and draped his great bare arm around my décolletée shoulders . . .
> But somehow as the winter drew on we did – I supposed by virtue of being the most dislocated members of that set – drift into a kind of spontaneous partnership. At evening parties we would bury ourselves in the same deep armchair sharing an inverted book. When other couples strolled past us we would break our habitual silence, concluding enigmatic remarks which, in our unwatched moments, we had not

troubled to begin. All of this must have come about naturally as if our predestined friendship had to pass laboriously through silence before creation . . .

'All your irony is assumed,' he whispered to me. 'You have really the heart of the romantic. Why will you not let me show you what life can be in the embrace of my boundless love? My one desire,' he continued, parting the ethereal green grapes that hung from my hat and burying his lips in my hair, my one desire is to be so very tender to you that you will smile without irony.' . . .

It was not only in his proportions that Colossus varied from the average man – but in the telescopic properties of those dimensions. He could push his entire consciousness into a wisp of grass, plunge his whole being through a dish of frost in a wheel rut – for when he halted to observe he seemed to leave his immeasurable carcass on the threshold of his interest. And when he had engulfed in his regard every pebble, every wish, every perpendicular of skyscraper, every metallic suspension and every square millimeter of the city he roamed in tenacious idleness – a sort of inquietude would invade his motor centers.

He was always looking for something of his own among all this – that something the poet always seems to have mislaid. He was occupied with identifying himself with every degree of height and depth – in that indescribable interchange he interrogated the earth in order to bear away as his seed. The secrets of the earth 're-minded' his creative will. He would hang for hours over splinters of quartz with their distinct diamantine resemblances until his eyes would glitter and reillumine their object . . .

I found him – the more I knew him – an utterly unprecedented biological and psychological enigma . . .

It is impossible, or at least dangerous, to remember Colossus after he left New York, for by this time I had magnified his being to such proportions that all comparisons vanished, which is the trick of falling in love. For him humanity drew its essential breath from an all-pervasive element superceding the air, the ether. Illimitable imbecility, spontaneous, irreducible, he foresaw in it the everlasting victor of our illusory intellection.[11]

Both Cravan and Mina Loy loved their dreams, including their super-impoverished marriage. As Cravan put it:

You must dream your life with great care
Instead of living it as merely an amusement.[12]

Cravan in all his guises was less a dream than a life, and he was Mina Loy's obsession for the major part of hers.

A radical statement begins issue 1: 'To Be or Not To Be . . . American'. We feel the hesitations and oppositions even through the irony. Again, we feel the relation to Pierre Albert-Birot's 'Nunism' or Nowism, to the ideas of Vitalism and Futurism: we might have the justified feeling that everything and everyone in Mina Loy's life relates to everything and everyone else. On that topic, here is a permit, ascribing to him the wrong birthplace: typical of much else about this more than remarkable character, unusual in every way. Everything wrong turns out to be right, for Cravan.

What a spoof, and exactly the kind of spoof Mina Loy will offer us in her satires of conversation among the 'cultured'

Arthur Cravan in Paris, 1908, photograph by F. Benedict.

groups at Mabel Dodge's Villa Curonia or at the Arensbergs in Manhattan. As Cravan wrote,

> It is essential to be American, or at least to look like you are one, which is exactly the same thing . . . In America, you are American only if you come from the United States, just as in France no one would reasonably think of themselves as French unless they came from Paris.[13]

His way of ending the piece is remarkably like Mina Loy's way of ending one of her conversational spoofs: 'Will you kindly shut up when I am talking,' pointing out as she speaks that she is speaking. When Cravan gets to the end of the talk, he makes himself the auto reference, whatever point he was making:

> Of late, it has become extremely fashionable to pass oneself off as a Negro.
> I would happily hold forth on this subject, but I fear to exhaust your patience – and myself.[14]

It is especially the 'NOTES' in *Maintenant* which manifest his brilliance about signatures and places and languages and dreams and names and epochs and prose poetry and just about everything else. The reader immediately feels the force of his dynamic assault. This typical phrase is characteristic of his forceful sallies: 'energy – concerning the dust of. emperors, I have had it in my eyes – '.[15]

And the journal continues with these enticing fragmented jottings called just NOTES (in *Maintenant*, translated by Terry Hale)

Had I known Latin at eighteen, I would have been Emperor
– Which is more nefarious: the climate of the Congo or genius? –

for a moment I thought of signing this Arthur the First –

I have dreamed of being great enough to found and fashion a republic all to. Myself . . . I have twenty countries in my memory and I drag the colours of a hundred cities in my soul –

I fight for breath equally (also) grit – my heart, break into a gallop –

Honest, I know myself for the creature and thief that I am –
My heart, break into a   gallop, I will be a millionaire – I wake a Londoner and go to bed an Asiatic – wind excites me
– I am always nervous –
I have also been the poet of destinies –

My art which is the most difficult because I adore it and I shit on it –
I am perhaps the king of failures because I'm certainly the king of something –

– It is me, your Cravan
    Wind
I feel the bloom of my youth and come fresh-faced
To admire America and its new cycle-racing tracks
My noble nature – astride a bicycle –

I am everything   any every inundation – after crying able to tear up my tears – I need a tremendous spree of debauchery – I am the child of my epoch – organism – I am what I am: the baby of an epoch. My heart shaken like a bottle – to pass with the utmost speed from enthusiasm to the most compete demoralization –

I am the beautiful Flora, Laurent de Médicis

I am Musset, Beethoven, the one who pulled the job in the rue des Reculettes –

Remember that my weight has often been my despair –

If I have a genius it is an exclusively humorous one, and I indisputably have a genius, and affirm that one often sees genius (the highest faculty to which man may attain according to the dictionary) that cannot be conceived of! – God, what an imbecile! –

And my weight is subject to tremendous fluctuation, my friends will tell you as much, my fleshy face becoming drawn in a matter of hours –

I feel reborn to a life of lies – to set my body. To music – to stuff my boxing-gloves with women's earrings – God is barking, we should open the door –

I am a caressing madman –[16]

Yes indeed! he wanted to be all-encompassing and that he was. What a madman, and what a grab-bag of notes caravanning after each other, so that the breathless reader can only tag along. Cravan was a genuine genius. 'I am a caressing madman' – perfectly put. Any page of his notes reveals much of his sort of joyous everywhichwayness of taking all things at the same level, the remembrance ('his memories dilated by beer') and his girth: 'his weight is subject to tremendous fluctuation,' but always quite weighty, so that he is impelled to laugh at someone who hasn't changed his weight in ten years. Much makes him laugh and blush! How impressive he is, the man of wit fighting in his nightshirt. Of course, these were Mina's earrings he stuffed into his boxing-gloves! This fits right along with Man Ray's substituting his thermometer to dangle down, at great length, for her earrings – all is humour in this crucial moment. I love his pointing out of the sceptic and the romantic in himself. For whom does he not take himself, being everyone? And at every moment, he takes himself for others: 'I am the beautiful Flora, Laurent de Médicis,' and also Musset, Beethoven. Strangely, it does not surprise us to find him as others – goodness knows, he was already naming himself many persons. Unsurprisingly, Mina Loy was also often changing her name, the beginning and the end. They so suited each other.

The refrains are as moving as they feel genuine: 'my heart, break into a gallop . . . My heart, break into a gallop' – the pace of the thing is extraordinary and the sweep no less so. The Londoner becomes the Asiatic, 'your Cravan' becomes the all: 'I am everything' and then the white space after that, to give the reader, and the speaker, time to fill that gap with anything we choose and he chooses. This is the kind of openness that Futurism was wanting, that Mina was always ready for, and I see it as just about the most crucial element of their being together: nothing was preordained, neither their getting together nor their wanderings, impoverished, through Mexico, and certainly not her setting off alone, carrying his child, nor his mysterious disappearance at sea. This was openness gone wild.

The king of something, surely, and perhaps of everything. The self-mockery ('God, what an imbecile!') is the other side, is as instantly recognizable as the self, inconceivably lofty despite the weight of the thing ('Remember that my weight has often been my despair'), and nevertheless, this is the body he sets to music. Even now, we hear this music, avidly, in all its brilliant notes.

Seen from Another Source[17]

Mina Loy's 'mystic Colossus' assumed this name on arriving in Paris in 1909, far before he encountered Mina. He was mystic because he was peculiar in all ways, enigmatic beyond belief, and about his birth and death there remain hanging many details. He called himself by multitudinous names, including 'the world's shortest-haired poet', and called others by insulting names, including Apollinaire ('the Jew Apollinaire', who was, of course, in no way Jewish) and Marie Laurencin ('Art is not a little pose in front of the mirror'). More enticing still is this postscript to a piece about the Salon des Indépendants: 'Being unable to defend myself against the critics who have hypocritically insinuated that I was related either to Apollinaire or to Marinetti, I hereby warn them that, if they repeat this, I shall twist their private parts.'[18]

Breton and Cravan

André Breton, an impassioned admirer of Cravan, insisted to Jacques Doucet, whose literary counsellor he was, that he purchase for his library all five numbers of *Maintenant*, adding that Jacques Vaché, whose *War Letters* he had already persuaded Doucet to buy, found the magazine highly entertaining. Georges Sebbag, in a piece labelled 'Arthur Cravan, the Nephew of Oscar Wilde', compares Jacques Vaché (who had, like Cravan, many names) to Jacques in Denis Diderot's *Jacques le Fataliste et son maître* and compares Rameau's nephew (in Diderot's *Le Neveu de Rameau*) to Cravan, Oscar Wilde's nephew, who recounts a visit (obviously, a fake visit) of the celebrated Wilde to himself, Arthur Cravan. It is convincing, as is the threesome Sebbag puts on stage: bringing them all to the Café de la Régence on the corner of rue St Honoré and the Place du Palais-Royal, the very same café where Nadja Léona (Delcourt) is meant to meet Breton, who got the wrong café.

Many meetings go on here, at great length, with long citations of Cravan's text in the fine translation by Terry Hale: 'I have lived in so many different milieux' and what Sebbag quite rightly calls Cravan's 'Philosophical theatre of the multiple'.[19] Thinking of all the aliases we have seen, here Sebbag is reminding himself and us that 'You have to "let yourself love all that you love / Accept yourself whole."'[20] The multiple personality now includes Arthur Rimbaud, and at this point, as at all the other points, nothing surprises us about either Cravan or Mina Loy.

Legends and Lasting

Those of us who have read and reread texts by and about Arthur Cravan are exhausted with the effort, rather like being in the boxing rings all those times when either, as in France, his assailants fell sick or didn't show, or, as in Barcelona and other Spanish points, he was soon defeated. We fall exhausted and are tempted to say: see which of his exploits strike you as the most fascinating – as they almost all are – and let yourself be captivated by your own multiple personalities. He provokes when he can: 'If I write, it is to annoy my peers, to make people talk about me, and to try to make a name for myself.'[21]

It never fails to amuse, if we have the kind of involvement in logopoeia that Pound ascribed to Mina Loy. We might find some nigh-fatal attraction to Cravan's sayings, in relation to his 'Visit to André Gide' (whose Lafcadio he inspired: see *Les Aventures de Lafcadio* or *Les Caves du Vatican*/The Vatican Cellars) where we find this kind of statement/question: 'it might be said that I have the morals of an Androgide. Will it be said?' Arthur Cravan was always fascinated by, haunted by, followed by the idea of suicide, that ultimate act for someone so inclined to staging himself. Mina Loy said of these frequent provocations that they were 'pantomimic atrocities on the spectator's habitual expectations . . . He worked to maintain his reality by presenting an unreality of himself to the world – to occupy itself with – which he made his spiritual getaway.'[22]

As Erich Weiss says in a book about *Maintenant*, Mina wrote to his mother Nellie Grandjean only three months after her arrival in Argentina. About his marriage with Mina (in the Basilica de Guadalupe), 'was a kind of modern one – for one

Arthur Cravan
during a boxing
exhibition, Tossa de
Mar, Spain, 1916.

Jack Johnson vs
Arthur Cravan, boxing
poster, April 1916.

year only'. Weiss finds it strange 'that he convinced his wife Mina Loy to abandon him in Mexico boarding a Japanese steamship as a nurse – heading for Argentina – where they intended to start a new life'. Was this an excuse? Legends last. Strange tales last.[23]

One of the most moving pieces about Cravan – and there are many – is by Alan Marshall, entitled 'The Ecstasy of Mina Loy', which takes up this disappearance. He associates the whole tale with the myth of Ariadne: Mina Loy is like Ariadne alone on the shore after the disappearance of Cravan. He also points out that 'as an artist, she always had Dionysus to fall back on' and Nietzsche's *Ecce homo* for inspiration. This ecstasy or 'perfect state of being outside yourself . . . [is such] a delight whose incredible tension sometimes triggers a burst of tears.'[24]

It is needless to say, yet I shall, that Cravan has had an immense influence on others, great Dada that he was: from early on, through the Surrealists like Robert Desnos, down to poets of today.[25] Desnos, in one of the trances for which he was famous, declaimed: 'Cravan bounds along the shore, his tie trailing in the wind' and then sketched a few signs marked 'The death of Cravan'.[26] Breton, in admiration, says of him: 'He managed, I believe, to be a deserter in five or six countries. As you can see, he was a curious man whose legend may well last. He disappeared a few years ago, trying to cross the Gulf of Mexico single-handed, on a stormy day, in a very frail boat.' Clearly this legend appealed to Breton, who gives him a high rank in the Anthology of Black Humour.[27] Cravan made a mark on Guy Debord and the Situationists, on Joseph Beuys, on Chris Burden and, of course, on his pal Marcel

Duchamp, who said: 'I knew him well and only Death can be the reason of Arthur's disappearance.'[28]

Mina Loy (right) with daughters Joella (left) and Fabienne (centre) at a carnival in Paris, 1925.

5

'THE WIDOW'S JAZZ': PARIS AGAIN

Mina was now forty, and looking much younger, as she usually did. She felt it peculiar, if interesting, to have rented a truly small apartment on 11 rue Campagne Première, right down the street from where she had lived with Stephen, undergone the birth of Oda Janet and mourned her so early death. It was full of good memories, like the next door Crèmerie Rosalie, with its wooden tables and benches where art students had gathered before the war. And famous residents, like Man Ray's Art Nouveau building at 31 bis, where he worked and lived with the model Kiki de Montparnasse, and whom we see in his film on the Robert Desnos poem *L'Etoile de mer*. Here she read of Giles' death of cancer at the age of fourteen, and here Joella came and agreed to sleep in Mina's bed to prevent her from self-harming in her intense melancholia over the news.

However, with her friends whom she met at cafés and gatherings and bookshops, like Sylvia Beach's Shakespeare & Company on the rue de l'Odéon, where she was a subscriber and where her books were exhibited, she wore a mask of cheerfulness. She was in fact part of 'the Crowd' whom Beach assembled around her, pointing out to others that there were three great beauties, all in the same family: Mina, Joella and Fabi. Beach also sympathized with Mina's situation of being doubly gifted: she had to be in the commercial world – thus making lampshades and hats quite like the lampshades and so needing a shop in which to sell them – and still find time to write her poems (and prose, always less well known). Mina took Joella to all these places, believing (in fact knowing) that one has to practise talking to all sorts of people in social gatherings.

Mina and Peggy and Natalie and Gertrude

Mina was wondering how to repay Peggy Guggenheim for a shop she had financed to provide her with a place to show her lampshades and other constructed objects. The shop, which Mina ran from 1925 to 1930, helped by Joella with the decoration and the management, was located at 52 rue de Colisée, a wealthy shopping district in Paris.[1] Here we can feel the extent of her worry as she asks Joella to 'treat' (interesting term!) the shop with her Christian Science, presumably to encourage some buyers.

The young American Julien Levy, fresh from Harvard, had come to France on the boat with Duchamp, who told him about Mina, and had hoped to make experimental films. But in order to have his rich father consent to Julien's marrying the lovely blonde Joella, to whom Robert McAlmon had introduced him, he had first to return to New York and his father's real estate business. Ironically, Julien and Joella were married at the same mairie of the Fourteenth Arrondissement where Mina had wed Stephen Haweis two decades before. When the couple left Paris for New York, Mina felt 'the most isolated godforsaken creature in Paris'.[2] Her poem 'The Widow's Jazz' has a sarcastic melody:

Cravan
colossal absentee

...

the widowed urn
holds impotently
your murdered laughter

...

Husband
How secretly you cuckolded me with death[3]

From time to time, she did indeed contemplate the possibility that Cravan had been murdered, but in any case, his mysterious disappearance wrought the same attack on her nerves and being as if he had indeed been murdered.

In the meantime, Natalie Barney's 'Académie des femmes' gathered all sorts of females, many of whom were to declaim dramatically like the great tragediennes of the nineteenth century, and her salon was the venue for famous events such as parts of Gertrude Stein's *The Making of Americans* being set to music by Virgil Thomson and translated by Mina into French. Mina became part of Natalie's circle and spent time with them all, including Djuna Barnes and also Dolly Wilde, 'Oscaria' ('I am more Oscar-like than he was himself') – who drank copiously and was addicted to cocaine. Djuna Barnes's *Ladies Almanack* of 1927–8 is a group portrait of this circle, with Mina, code-named Patience, insisting that to have two genders is far more interesting than to have only one. How this speaks to our moment!

Mina's shop and her output of lamps were prospering now, with some shades in a cellophane called Crystal Luc. A new synthetic material, Rhodoid, was good for the floral forms she was

Mina Loy and Djuna Barnes, New York, 1920, photograph by Man Ray.

good at shaping and for her other styles, like her 'imageries lumineuses', those light-filled objects like fairy tales for grown-ups, and her way of summoning the stars and a dance of the constellations. Her double attraction to the earth and the sky during her entire life, augmented by her genuine attachment to Christian Science, contributed to the interested public the opposite of the severe lines of the contemporary designs.

Her Paris life could be well summed up, in some of its phases, by the word 'intensity'. In Mina Loy's being, there was always a concordance between her poetically intense self and her personal intensity.

Mina Loy's passport photograph, 1920s.

Mina's Intensity

A remarkable poem of this period, entitled 'There Is Neither Life nor Death', was composed by Mina at some point in the year 1914–15:

> There is no Life or Death
> Only activity
> And in the absolute
> Is no declivity.
> Only propensity
> Is a nonentity.
> There is no First or Last
> Only equality
> And who would rule
> Joins the majority.
> There is no Space or Time
> Only intensity,
> And tame things
> Have no immensity.[4]

This remarkably rhyming poem makes its point precisely because of all the repetitiveness, which would not continue in Mina's work, and so is all the more striking as an assault on tameness and bourgeois niceness. That very characteristic intensity is the one quality that predominates in the manifestations of Futurism and Dada, the kind of attitude and universe she would inhabit during the encounter with the over-the-top Cravan from 1916 until 1917. In no way was this a tame meeting between two tame people: rather the opposite.

'The Widow's Jazz': Paris Again

Group portrait of American and European artists outside Le Jockey, Montparnasse, Paris, 1923. Back row, left to right: Bill Bird, unknown, Holger Cahill, Lee Miller, Les Copeland, Hilaire Hiler, Curtis Moffat. Middle row: Kiki de Montparnasse, Margaret Anderson, Jane Heap, unknown, Ezra Pound. Front row: Man Ray, Mina Loy, Tristan Tzara, Jean Cocteau.

We can hear Harriet Monroe thinking about it in Paris in 1923, with McAlmon and Ezra Pound. She writes: 'A great deal of this gayety and color aforesaid was due to the presence of Mina Loy. Her personality is quite irresistible... Yes, poetry is in this lady whether she writes it or not.'[5]

6

INSEL, 1933–6

This enormously bizarre and un-worked-over attempt at a novel was originally seen as part of a larger narrative called 'Islands in the Air'. It is at once 'an autobiographical, fictional, orthogonal alternative to established genres', as Elizabeth Arnold, who rescued it from the passive archive of unpublished material in the Beinecke Library, terms it.[1] The problem for me is not the alternating American and English spellings, which Mina Loy used interchangeably, but the rather dragging pace of the understandably incomplete text.

It is based on the temperament and life of Richard Oelze, Surrealist, who was in Paris from 1933 until 1936 along with Mina Loy, who was herself involved with this odd character. He was at times large, at times shrivelled, and was known to be, as Arnold puts it, a 'misanthropic surrealist'. When Mina Loy put aside this book, she declared: 'I feel there's something wrong – & all the same time something right – I can't see it yet from the other side.'[2] Yes indeed. There may in fact have been for her, as there is for me, no other side. Let me say, once and sort of for all, that I now see it as an effort not worth the time of reading or of Mina Loy's writing, and that I however feel obliged to deal with it as I can. She could be taken in so strangely and for such a brilliant woman and writer and painter and constructor, it seems odd, but we all have been taken in at some point. It is therefore instructive, and I am relating my experience of this, in honour of Mina Loy, but it is an obligation.

This 'novel' is, as we follow the pages, a story about a 'more or less surrealist painter, who, although he had nothing to eat, was hoping to sell a picture to buy a set of false teeth'. This is because he longs to go to a brothel, but doesn't want to disgust a prostitute by his ugliness. To read his description, we tend to think he was right about wanting to change something, for his face is like a death's head, and seems to be mixed up with black magic. 'They will grin and there is nothing but a skull peering at you, at once it's all over – but you remember.'[3]

The description continues, and it is certainly the most impressive thing about this text, for his queer and ash-coloured face was like the rest of his pitiful body: 'his torso so concave, he was so emaciated that from his waist down he looked like a stork on one leg.'[4] There must have been some attraction for Mina, we suppose, in his ironical assessment of his own work, even if it is unattainable for us in this creepy text: 'He varnished his painting of the past with a gentle irritation of commentarial laughter.'[5] (He was incredibly impoverished, and we see over and over how Mina Loy was compassionate in all her writings – those finished and those unfinished – towards the impoverished. Insel (I am now wondering if the title indicates In Itself) was housed in a village already 'dismantled' and would sneak out at dark in search of a remnant of something edible, and this might well remind the reader of the Bowery bums and the poet's compassion for them.

If we try to care about this text or why it should have been rescued, we might want to learn that Insel's father was a *Schlosser*, a blacksmith, and so his destiny was mixed up with keys. We think of Mina Loy's father, not a blacksmith but a tailor; in any case involved in an existence laudable for its persistence in times of stress. So Insel thinks of Kafka, as a 'foreshadowing of my hounded existence, recognized by the relentless drive of my peculiar misfortune'. The meeting of extremes pictures the highs and lows of Oelze's self-maintenance as a writer and self-picturer: 'If he was a lunatic, he was prodigious.' As a kind of autobiographer, 'he was continually dressing up his insanity in another man's madness.'[6]

In this world, as in Mina Loy's and often our own, everybody was always 'writing something'. It is a familiar world to many of us, with elements that at least want to be interesting: there are not just paintings, but 'photographs of paintings'. A sort of irony plays over the writing, in its interrogations of the 'artist' in the text, at times of Mina Loy the painter herself:

> 'whose pictures are these?'
> 'Who could have done these?'
> 'They are mine.'
> 'You are an extraordinarily gifted woman,' he said.

So the genders are mixed, and the confusion should give it some spirit. 'Ah, my book is "not like those pictures". My last exhibition, he said, was "cancelled the moment the dealer set eyes on them".'[7] And indeed, he was helplessness personified. Here appears once more Mina Loy's compassion for the out-of-luck, and her lyric style of her caring:

> Whenever I have seen poor people asleep on stone seats in the snow, there arise in my mind unused ballrooms and vacationers' apartments whose central heating warms a swarming absence.[8]

We notice, as is habitual with all Mina Loy's writings, the interior rhyme: 'warm/swarming'. The narrator feels impelled to disencumber it from its 'personalia' – just too much of that over-lean man. There is, and this is part of the personalia, in Insel's habitual jumble, a subconscious 'arrangement', whatever that might mean in such a mind. It is given over, it seems, to the 'degradation of women', which inflicts an acute pain; with all the 'deadly detail, the mind disintegrates'. That is, presumably, both minds: that of the mad Surrealist painter, and that of the narrator. Moreover, we can't help feeling, abused as we are by the abundance of everything trivial, a threat to the reader. This text feels to me like a thing better left in an unpublished state...

Now, that remark of mine would qualify as adverse, and the text itself points out something on the topic: 'Adverse remarks with ordinary men it is politic to keep to oneself while to withhold one's comments from Insel would have appeared impolite.' The reason being that his entire self takes 'the form of a question mark'.[9]

Not that the dreaded madman takes up all the space in this book: there enter Man Ray and other notable real persons, such as Simon Legree and Raoul Dufy, as well as cultural references. Our own minds feel invaded by the narration of all the varying states of consciousness imposed by 'this uncommon derelict'. That is in fact the best description of Insel, who is far from ordinary persons and absolutely derelict in all the senses of the word. Interestingly, his tramp's wardrobe, we hear later, consists of a white handkerchief and a white comb.

It becomes well nigh impossible to understand some paragraphs. Try this one about a simple act of our everyday lives, we would think, except that here it connects with ancient temples and their rituals, like descending the stairs backwards so as to avoid the deity's power for the negative, leading directly to this relatively impenetrable statement: 'So the shutting of doors is a concentration of our radiations in rectangular containers to economize the essences of our being we dispense to those with whom we communicate.'[10] (Not so much communication in this place, but we have at least an agreeable setting, like the terrace of the Hotel Lutetia, and an equally agreeable brandy.)

Furthermore, we cannot accuse Insel of lying, for this seems both a simple statement and a true one: 'I'm so ugly naked.' And later, the narrator feels herself always propping him up, with 'his immovable eyes glued to infinity', and laying him down, not in a bed, rather under a 'canopy of poverty', or finally in a box under one of the bridges over the Seine. We again imagine the Bowery bums, even in this Paris we recognize as 'something known which, in spite of life, we would know again'. Then the Gare d'Orléans offers a stage for Insel 'to unroll his increate existence to the fitting applause' of departures and the noise of feet thumping along.

Some of the descriptions of this mad artist ring true: 'He had always something about him of a lithe tree struck by its own lightning ... And all the while Insel spasmodically kept up his bums's charade pleading for variable salvations.'[11] All Loy's bums merge in our memory as real creatures, pitiable and capable of arousing her real spirit, for she seems untouched by what we call 'compassion fatigue'. When he sets himself on fire 'his astounding vibratory flux' prevents a normal inflagration, for he gives off an infrared or invisible ray. 'So one saw him as a gray man and an electrified organism at one and the same time.'[12] Then he pulls off his face, and we will leave him there for the moment, while later, he will assert himself in a complete reversal. 'I am eternally content. My happiness is infinite. All the desires of the earth are consummated within myself.' And then, all of a sudden, the narrator disintegrates, with a life-force blasting her apart, placing her in Insel's situation, suffused by 'mental hilarity'.

Now appears the spectre of Mina Loy's lost beloved Arthur Cravan, whose face in a photograph aroused the admiration of Insel:

> Swift as the leaves of the shutter on a camera when a snapshot is taken, there came together upon his concentric face a distinct enlargement of Colossus' photograph that always stood on the sitting room mantelpiece at the other end of the flat.

Insel on his first visit had taken that photo between his hands to stare at it inordinately as if for reproduction, for a long time, remarking: 'Such beauty as this could scarcely happen more than once in a hundred years.'

We are permitted to stare at objects here and are privileged, above all, to encounter a description by this lampshade artist of something precise:

a pattern of a 'detail' to be strewn about the surface of clear lamp shades. Through equidistant holes punched in a crystalline square, I had carefully urged in extension, a still celluloid coil of the color that Schiaparelli has since called shocking pink. Made to be worn around pigeon's ankles for identification, I had picked it up in the Bon Marché.

The narrator offers the madman a little box he desires,

> a small object by the American surrealist, Joseph Cornell, the delicious head of a girl in slumber afloat with a night light flame on the surface of water in a tumbler, of bits cut from early Ladies' Journals (technically in pupilage to Max Ernst), in loveliness, unique in Surrealism – the tidal lines of engraving cooled its static peace. Under the glass lid a slim silver slipper and a silver ball and one of witch's blue came raining down on the gray somnolence when one lifted it up.

Their final meeting takes place in the Capoulard's Café, and she speaks: 'Of course,' I was saying, 'I don't know where you are – wherever it is is very far away. And I am just as far away. I have existed before my time.'[13] Criticizing his idea of suffering for love as sheer slush, she announces for him and us readers the end of their meeting:

> It had taken so short a time for this parting of the ways to subdivide into the thousand directions. Yet even now he was rich in postponements.
>
> . . .
>
> Nothingness.

Capoulards Café: which reminds us of the 'Café du Néant', that poem about Papini and facing him across the table as the affair is ending. She admits her own endless incompletions, even as she deceives herself, answering Insel's question as to how her book is going:

> 'It is going wonderfully,' . . . belatedly believing I had reached the stage prescribed by Colossus for creation, when all that one has collected rolls out with the facility of the song of a bird.[14]

Realizing that his radioactivity would have to give out, she tells us how she departed: 'So all I said was -bye.' And describes his 'bittersweet stare both dazed and stoic as he says just "Danke fur alles" – thanks for everything.'[15] She sees the café clock gratefully as a reminder of the temporal.

There are two essays in the *Salt Companion to Mina Loy* I enjoyed consulting in the case of *Insel*, with which I needed help, finding it next to unreadable. By some peculiar irony, I was attempting to grapple with it in a visit to Aspen, Mina's final home. In Sandeep Parmar's piece, I read that *Insel* signals the 'failure of the avantgarde to prophesy or prevent the approaching reality of wars' and manifests the 'Absolute presence or "hereness" of one being, and this hereness is identical with the hereness of all beings of all time.'[16] And David Ayers's 'Mina Loy's *Insel* and Its Contexts' summed it up as being an older woman, a younger man and a gradual shift in emotional power relations between them, and between economics and creativity, and the relation of all this to Paris, art and Surrealism in the mid-1930s. He shows Insel as a healer, in a kind of mesmerism, as 'his personal power

– as electricity, magnetism, aura or rays increases in proportion to his physical decay.' He also points out, as I should have guessed, that this writing was too Surrealist for the Surrealists, 'a lost classic of drug literature alongside Burroughs' and Alastair Crowley. Amusingly, he sees Lewis Carroll among the more 'subdued presences in Insel: his Cheshire Cat, a model for Insel's autonomous mouth, disembodied smile, mouthless cats'. And a sort of relation to the story of *Nadja*.[17] Right on.

Elizabeth Arnold, who had the courage to edit this to me almost unreadable volume, tells us how it is a novel written by a poet, that is, because of the sound of words. And it very much reminds us of Ezra Pound speaking of Loy's 'logopoeia', the words mattering more than anything. To be sure, this is about an ethereal bum, mysterious but far less interesting to me than the angel bums of that wonderful long poem 'Hot Cross Bum'.

INTERVAL: MINA LOY THE ARTIST

Mina Loy's early sketches and paintings were astonishingly unlike her later work. We see a decorative butterfly lightness, or a sort of parody of the Pre-Raphaelites, and elsewhere Art Deco flourishes full of nymphs and flowering shrubs, as if she were decorating one of the Italian or Parisian cafés or salons and then the New York equivalent.

Take, for example, the very early *Teasing a Butterfly* (1902), whose angelic faces are remarkably awful. That term does not only apply to the faces, monstrous with staring eyes, rather like spiders. For this is to say nothing of the hands, like so many scary Halloween imprints, placed on the support and as if right up against our observers' faces, and not exactly teasing either. As so often in Mina Loy's works, both visual and verbal, the contrast of the title with the actual text or image is startling, for here we see no tease, just a nightmare gone luminous.

This is presumably a dreaming vision, with the face of the dreamer, on the far bottom right corner, in shadow and the ghastly vision illuminated. This is a typical case of the title gone askew, probably on purpose. Mina Loy had, among other things in her quite bizarre personality, an impulse towards the odd. Then there is the extraordinary *Love Caressed by the Lovely Ladies/*

Mina Loy, *Teasing a Butterfly*, 1902, oil on canvas.

Mina Loy, *Dawn*, c. 1903, oil on board.

Mina Loy, *Fallen Angels*, c. 1903, oil on board.

L'Amour dorloté par les belles dames of 1906, with the figures very much in the Symbolist mode. And from the same year, with the same sorts of figures, this Gothic rendering of a strange narrative full of yearning and a mockery of religious imagery. This is Mina Loy in her young and brilliant mode, which produced also in 1903 the rather frightful *Dawn* and the rearing snails of the *Fallen Angels*.

When the Salon d'Automne opened in 1903 and exhibited some of her works, Mina took the name Loy, stating that she was – as indeed she was always – a law (*loi*) unto herself. In the 1906 Salon, she attracted the attention of a critic in the *Gazette des Beaux-Arts*: 'Mlle Mina Loy in whose uncommon watercolours Guys, Rops and Beardsley are combined.' The reference is to that *Love Caressed by the Lovely Ladies*, a flouncy sort of work, and a

Stephen Haweis and Mina Loy in their Paris studio, *c.* 1905, photograph by Henry Le Savoureux.

Interval: Mina Loy the Artist

Photograph of Mina Loy's Mappamundo.

complicated satire full of sexual innuendos that is especially interesting if we compare it with her satires of the conversations of the cultural salon. This is a remarkably unsettling and suffocating scene. These creations create an uneasy setting. Uneasy all over.

Then there are works with the same uncomfortably Gothic figures, like *The Paper House*, a drawing and gouache also of 1906. There is a story behind this, as often behind Mina's works in all genres, with a sort of religious pilgrimage and a worshipping maiden. Gothic gone mad, I would say – but brilliant.

Stephen Haweis, photographer and portrait painter, who at the start of their relationship was as enthusiastic about his photography as she was about whatever she was doing, took an interest in her work for a while. He indeed took magnificent photographs of her, and these remain with us, as do her sumptuous ways of looking. With her usual ease and elegance, she seemed to float about in the visual realm as easily as in that of the conversational, with a string of admirers we cannot wonder at, her hair parted in the centre as no one else could wear it, her jewellery just right for the frocks she concocted for herself and the hats she concocted for others, under the name of Schiaparelli or her own.

Mina Loy, *L'Amour dorloté par les belles dames*, 1906, drawing and gouache.

Mina Loy, *Self-Portrait*, c. 1905, pencil on paper laid on cardboard.

Or then the lampshades she concocted over the years: for her inventiveness extended far into realms no other brain had imagined or indeed could envision. I am thinking of the flowery lampshades of early on, the aeroplane lampshade of 1941, and her global-thinking *Mappamondo* so wide-ranging in their imagination. Whenever we see them, they light up our views of the painter and poet and inventor she was. To such an extent was she at once outside and inside herself that she could dress as a lampshade, say, in 1917, for the Blindman's Ball, and in addition, picking back up on this talent now and then, almost make a living from selling them.

Here she is with Peggy Guggenheim in 1926 in a lamp shop Peggy financed, with paintings by Peggy's then husband, Lawrence Vail, on the wall. Although the shop could be marked 'Mina Loy', Peggy had her own not altogether admirable reasons for financing the enterprise. It seems that never did Mina tire of inventing such luminous objects: in fact, one of the biggest reaches within a creation's title is the 'celestial globe lamp', and the French poster advertising her fairy-like shades as 'L'ombre féerique' shows the idea itself: light and shadow mingled magically. So the lamp shop at 52 rue du Colisée was meant to, and did, say just what it meant to say and show: 'Lamps in old glass and new shades.' (Mina Loy illuminated not only the mental capacity of the Parisian public by her poems, but their actual physical surroundings. This talent surpassed any simple decorative doing.)

I see this as early Mina, not so different from the later one, in which she was able to preserve her sense of the comic along with her sense of the illuminated theatricality possible in art. Now I should avoid using the appellation 'artist' too loosely, for

Mina Loy (seated) and Peggy Guggenheim (standing) in the lamp shop at
52 rue Colisée, Paris, c. 1926.

my beloved and elegant friend Jacqueline Lamba would insist I never use that characteristic 'artist' for her being or endeavours: they were paintings, and she was a painter. The lesson impressed itself upon me strongly.

Mina's inventiveness served her well, always, from the lampshade shop she ran with her daughter Joella (before Joella's departure for New York with her husband Julien Levy, whose representative in Paris Mina became), to her membership, if that is the appropriate term, of the Arensberg salon, where her

Photograph of Mina Loy's Calla Lily lamp.

Poster for the Blindman's Ball, 25 May 1917, with a drawing by Beatrice Wood.

Mina Loy dressed for the Blindman's Ball, 1917.

impressive large brooches and necklaces would give off just the right note. And in her later years at Aspen, after she moved there to be near her daughters and their husbands, her long frocks, sometimes velvet, that she had designed and made, down to her ankles and her slippers – making her walking not exactly easy – were constantly remarked upon, from all we can tell, appreciatively, even admiringly, and rarely depreciated.

She was unusual, to put it mildly, but admirable. Here is where anyone of a less firm character would have verged on the absurd. Her very peculiarity was priceless, and this could be said of any of the periods through which she so intensely lived: her youth in London and the bizarreries of the Munich art world, and her involvement with Stephen, with Gertrude Stein, Apollinaire and the art crowd, the Parisian and New York scenes (having left her two children in Florence for two years), her Bowery years and then Aspen . . . Each time we see her as herself in whatever get-up she has chosen. The famous photographs of Mina Loy as this gorgeous creature or that, and Stephen's famous portrait, never fail to do her justice. Here is Lee Miller's grand portrait of her from 1930.

After marvelling (not always happily) at the change in her appearance from this time to that, it seems to me that she was never 'striking a pose' but rather inhabiting her own personality. Moreover, this seems true even as she was acting a part, as in the theatre with the Provincetown Players. Alfred Kreymborg had written a one-act play, *Lima Beans*, and offered her the part of the wife, while the poet and doctor William Carlos Williams was to play the husband, and William Zorach, the set designer, was to play a vegetable huckster as the third member of the cast. The wife was to serve, by her own decision, string rather than

Mina Loy, *c.* 1930, gelatin silver print, photograph by Lee Miller.

Mina Loy and William Carlos Williams in *Lima Beans*, Alfred Kreymborg's 'scherzo for marionettes' play, as staged at the Provincetown Playhouse, December 1916.

lima beans, and the three-person cast was to perform like marionettes, the couple holding hands as if woodenly, coached by Kreymborg wielding a baton. The play was written in rhythmical free verse; the kitchen was designed by Kreymborg like a chessboard and the curtain decorated with vegetables. A bit unusual even for the venturesome players, but most interesting for us, the part was always clearly Mina Loy, fine actress as she was. She was wearing a décolleté green taffeta gown, gold slippers on her gorgeous legs and her self-designed jewellery, including a mosaic brooch and dangling gold earrings, much admired by Marianne Moore in the audience.

Mina herself wrote very short Futurist-style playlets, one called *Collision*, with an orator and a vibrating set with its 'planes and angle of wall and ceiling' interchanging as in a kaleidoscope; another was *Cittàbapini* (alluding to her affair with Papini) and a third *The Pamperers*, which included bits of conversation overheard on the street, again so very avant-garde, like the poetry of

Guillaume Apollinaire with its collaged elements from the actual world.¹ The playlets, brief and bizarre, appeared in *Rogue* thanks to Carl Van Vechten. Her Futurist past left its traces everywhere, or almost. Mina Loy was never to lose an opportunity, or very seldom, for which we readers remain grateful.

She would be happy one day to find herself at the Arensbergs in such company, particularly since she greatly liked Arensberg's 'To a Poet', calling God 'the great Cosmical Non-entity', and Louise Norton's 'Philosophic Fashions' by 'Dame Rogue'. Her New York time had been well prepared for. Another side of her encounter with Futurism was rearoused by the wartime impossibility of female participation in the battlefield. Her 'feminine politics' was never much in abeyance, and the 'Sex War' was never extant. As in Futurism, men and women were 'intimate irritants'.²

Man Ray's delightful picturing of her with a thermometer instead of earrings says it all: she could be teased and he could certainly tease. For the latter action, we have only to look at the mockery she was to make of the Futurists in Florence (those 'Flabberbags') and of the salons she frequented. She was fond of Man Ray, and her portrait of him in pencil is memorable.

Mina Loy, *Marianne Moore*, n.d., pencil on paper.

Mina Loy, *c.* 1920, photograph by Man Ray.

Mina Loy, *Man Ray*, c. 1925, pencil on paper.

The Act of Art

Mina Loy knew how to look, what to look at and what was worth representing in art, poetry and the world around her. She greatly enjoyed Brancusi's welcome to his studio, with other artists and thinkers and poets: here he is with Tristan Tzara, Jane Heap and Margaret Anderson, along with the glamorously bearded Brancusi. Here is her 1922 contemplation of Brancusi's 'Golden Bird' – that quite extraordinary bronze statue – a soaring response to the implied flight and the corresponding depth of its conception. This poem stretches out in our imagination, without the length of Loy's long poems like *Anglo-Mongrels and the Rose* and the bumhood poem 'Hot Cross Bum'.

> The toy
> Become the aesthetic archetype
>   As if
> some patient peasant God
> had rubbed and rubbed
> the Alpha and Omega
> of Form   into a lump of metal

Of course that form takes a capital F, and the 'lump' has to be rubbed for the Forming of this element into the archetype that some exotic god has concocted, 'as if'. And so, without unnecessary detail, the majestic procession of the poem's envisioning unfolds from a token of play ('toy') to the 'archetype' already forefigured. How beautiful is the stark absence of wings and feathers, even as the 'crest and claw' lead towards the final soaring gesture.

Interval: Mina Loy the Artist

Brancusi, Tristan Tzara, Berenice Abbott, Mina Loy, Jane Heap and Margaret Anderson in Brancusi's studio, 8 Impasse Ronsin, Paris, 1923, gelatin silver print.

At the centre of this very great poem, an absolute bareness is crucial to any revelation. This *conformation*, and its implicit confirmation, serve as an example of how Mina Loy's wordplay manages to pick up the already presented Form that makes the 'lump' into the act of art. This transformation is saluted by the trumpeting sound of the repeated 'c' – as the poet's affection for sound sometimes declares itself loudly. We notice there is no pause or capitalization marking the space between these two shouting stanzas:

The absolute act
of art
conformed
to continent sculpture
– bare as the brow of Osiris –
this breast of revelation

an incandescent curve
licked by chromatic flames
in labyrinths of reflections

Suddenly we hear the gong pounded, struck and sounded beyond the pure aesthetic of the opening stanza into an extreme hyper-consciousness of repetition. The observer or reader suffers the poetic violence of the resounded sibilant 's' stretching to the limits of audible credibility:

(shrill/aggressive/strikes/significance)
This gong
of polished hyperaesthesia
shrills with brass
as the aggressive light
strikes
its significance

This procession in the perfect brassiness of the bronze moves towards the conclusion in a religious ritual celebrating the mute 'inaudible bird' in its final modesty. Its gorgeous non-showiness is further stressed by incompletion, the three dots of inconclusiveness: as Gertrude Stein had said, Mina Loy was able

Joseph Cornell, *Mina Loy*, 1930s, box with Man Ray photograph of Mina Loy, c. 1920.

Mina Loy, *Christ on a Clothesline*, c. 1955–9, collage and mixed media.

to grasp the meaning of a text without its punctuation, and didn't need commas or any other 'normal' signalling system. She was a poetic genius, and precisely if ironically (and she was an absolute mistress of irony) she said she was no poet. This is *not* the work of no poet, no matter how 'reticent' that announcement. Thomas Merton, the monk of silence and poetic contemplation, admired the work of Mina Loy, just as Joseph Cornell, himself a kind of monk of construction, admired her work and her being. They communed – not on that communal cot in the Bowery's manifestation of ultimate and enforced material poverty, but in the other real world of the poem itself. The capitalized beginning of the final stanza makes an announcement of immaculate flight in its initial magnificence:

> The immaculate
> conception
> of the inaudible bird
> occurs
> in gorgeous reticence . . .[3]

In that remarkable almost-oxymoron of gorgeous reticence, we sense the distinctive talent of Mina Loy, artist and perceiver.

The Epic View

Two of her paintings strike us immediately as the most powerful possible statements of misery related to poverty, loneliness and her long poem of heart-scathing pain, 'Hot Cross Bum'. These are epic paintings in relation to the epic poem, and I shall put them alongside each other.

One of Mina Loy's most moving and terrible pieces of imagining, rooted in my mind forever now, is *Christ on a Clothesline*, for there he hangs, whatever religion one holds to or not. Thomas Merton was right in his salute to Mina Loy, and how the real and the suffering work together here, as she uses the face of a Scandinavian fisherman to be the face of Christ, says more than anyone could ever say about Mina Loy's knowledge of the reality of suffering. It is reminiscent of her *Wooden Madonna*, which Mina sculpted when her child Oda died just after her first birthday, and Mina sat up all night long to make it. It takes longer than that for this hanging to subside in the visual imagination.

She mingles satire and compassion throughout her depictions of the figures in the brief and unforgettable prose of 'Street Sister' and in these other poems, the magnificent and melancholy

Mina Loy, *Communal Cot*, c. 1950, papier maché and rags.

Interval: Mina Loy the Artist

Marcel Duchamp inspects *Bums Praying* in Mina Loy's Stanton Street apartment, c. 1959.

figures in their contrary ways, dancing and slumping, looking upwards somehow in whatever circumstances we find them or read them. This is surely the way that poetry knows how to salute poverty and genius, as they mingle, as she does entirely in the configuration of her great epic poem of 1945, miraculously entitled 'Hot Cross Bum'.

And here, in close conjunction to *Christ on a Clothesline*, I want to place Mina Loy's invaluable and unforgettable tragic piece *Communal Cot*, which lies beside that great epic poem.

In relation to this epic poem, I have been thinking of the importance of the detail within an epic length. Surely, there is not anything massively heroic in the selling of the smallish bun, and yet there is a massive amount of parody in the 'Bums for Buns'. But what a grand bright red lurid drunken modern-lit opening prepares the 'bonfire of the soul' and the 'kindling of the eyes' for the Inferno of the Babylon of the Bowery!

> Beyond a hell-vermillion
> curtain of neon
> lies the Bowery
>
> a lurid lane
> leading misfortune's monsters
>
> the human . . . race
> altered to irrhythmic stagger
>
> along the alcoholic's
> exit to Ecstasia.

These monsters are not more monstrous than man, as this strange long poem moves on from the punning of buns and bums,

> Bum-bungling of actuality
>   exchanging
>   an inobvious real
> for over-obvious irreal

As if by a miracle, amid the drastic consumption of cheap wine, and the tourist attraction of such a scene, there is suddenly

> an onfall
> of somewhat heavenly loaves

>   for your loafing
>   is the fashion
>
>   conditional compassion
>   appreciation
>   of your publicity value
>   to the Bowery
>
>   So here comes help
>   here comes regeneration
>   – even a little alimentary fun
>   you shall not be left in the lurch
>
>   Some passing church
>   or social worker
>
>   confides to a brother
>   how he has managed to commandeer
>   a certain provision
>   of hot-cross buns

Those bells we will be hearing from Brancusi's fellow Romanian Tristan Tzara's epic *Approximate Man* sound here as the fire recurs hellishly:

>   a dull-dong bell
>   thuds out admonishment
>   to worship
>   . . .
>   whose cadence

of illenience
transforms the cross bewailed
to flammable timber
for over-heating
Hades

waylaying for branding
indirigible bums
with the hot-cross
of ovenly buns.

Among the ash-cans and their ritual offering of offal, the scraps
of humans and their consumption remain scattered.

And always on the trodden street
– the communal cot –

embalmed in rum
under an unseen
baldachin of dream
blinking his inverted sky
of flagstone

prone
lies the body of the flop
where'er he drop.

One still savors
the favor of Eros

> In this sore cemetery of the Comatose
> here lies . . .

The final play of the Comatose and Eros ends with an incoming tide of the alcoholic, vagabonding and mad-erotic wanderer, as he exults in acting out a violent last bodily jab:

> A vagabond in delirium
> aping the rise and fall
>
> of ocean
> of inhalation
> of coition.[4]

The ending is erotically transforming and monstrously human, as the angelic bums receive the bread to go with their wine for their communion on the communal cot, a sustenance envisioned and real.

Mina Loy and Joseph Cornell

Joseph Cornell, shy, gaunt and certainly a genius like Mina Loy, had an exhibition of his bird boxes, called *Aviary*, at the Egan Gallery in New York City, then recreated in 2018 at the Metropolitan Museum, which was mobbed by visitors. This recalled the bearded and elegant Brancusi's utterly simple *Bird in Space* of 1923. Mina had painted her friend Brancusi and was doubly close with Cornell since both were faithful Christian Scientists. Cornell was a faithful attendee at the church on Wednesdays, and firmly believed in the teachings of Mary Baker Eddy, whose

Constantin Brancusi, *Bird in Space*, 1923, marble sculpture.

Science and Health with Key to the Scriptures was his resource for his life.

When I was preparing my Joseph Cornell book on his diaries and source files, I had to ask written permission of the Mother Church in Boston for permission to publish Cornell's letters to his mother and his invalid brother, both of whom had departed and thus might seem strange recipients to non-believers. Cornell and Mina Loy hit it off perfectly, given their joint belief in the good and the pure, devoid of the 'deviltries' – as Cornell would put it –of some works of modern art. And this fitted perfectly: Mina Loy was convinced, or wanted to be, that, as Christian Science would have it, 'Evil doesn't exist.' So, as with the Bowery Bums, the emaciated faces haven't cruelty in them, and the face of Christ hanging on that clothesline – the visage of that Scandinavian fisherman she used – is pure in its haggardness.

As opposed to evil and black magic, 'white magic' is what Cornell cared to be and wanted to be always about, and those boxes, in one of which he has portrayed Mina Loy, are out to capture the best of performance: the ballerinas and the singers are always stars, subject for admiration. Cornell had seen her paintings a decade earlier, and had found them 'evoking at times certain commonplace experiences with amazing vividness and unbelievable pleasure'.[5] For both of them, and for the Christian Science they practised, it was and is the phenomena of each day in its details that matter and impart pleasure.

On top of that, Loy's poems and prose in her *Lunar Baedeker* could have been designed by their title and their summoning up of the moon to appeal to this wiry artist, who rose before dawn every day to read his Christian Science lesson. He thought of her lunar imagination in those dark but luminous moments, and their both being Capricorns further played into their mental intimacy. The notes he passed her on blue paper furthered this cross-cutting of celestial images. She often had in mind his creating a kind of heaven in his image chambers, a kind of poetics of construction, as her own turned out to be.

In September 1953 Cornell sent her a message about T. S. Eliot (writing as T. S. Apteryx in *The Egoist*) having said of her poetry that 'She needs the support of the image, even if only as the instantaneous point of departure' and that some of her too-abstract poems permit the word to separate from the thing. An interesting observation, for indeed it sometimes feels to the reader that a Mina Loy poem is overly abstract, and not anchored in the real – which is of particular importance for both Cornell and Mina Loy, both of whose 'scientific attitude' (that is, of Christian Science) has a perspective on the 'real' with its issue in the transcendent other reality. This is, to say the least, somewhat different from the perspective of Eliot, an Anglican by choice, who had a different take on the real.

In September 1946, Cornell sent her a typical letter about his doings and about his being. They valued each other immensely, as much in their correspondence makes clear, without sentimentality.

> FLORAL STILL-LIFE: (first version of letter to Mina Loy)
> Dear Mina,
> Autumn seems to be in such a quandary this year.
> And why am I writing to you about the weather? BECAUSE yesterday afternoon, hung about with mist, a really ambiguous afternoon for Fall, I came across a smoked-fish delivery truck parked on the shabby fringe of a shopping center near us. On

the side of this small vehicle painted on enseigne in the form of a still life of various stock, fat pieces of meat surmounted by whole fish in colours that make one think it might at one time have been a bright decalcomania, silvery whites and greys against the erring color of the cross sections. Viewed close up, the background sky blue betrayed beneath the black lettering of a former, less picturesque, version of trade-mark. The effect as shabby and uninspired as the afternoon.

What I am leading up to is the lesson in INSPIRATION that shabby little enseigne held for me. For I glimpsed that MOTION exactly two years ago for the first time on a beautifully clear shining day on a ride to an unfamiliar section near the water wonderfully evocative of the American past in the unfolding rural panorama, creative in its nostalgia and mellowness.

I arose at four this morning and a little later typed this with my back against the open gas oven. It is now six thirty, misty sharp, and a tiny crescent moon gleaming through a forest of silhouetted branches against the horizon becoming faintly blue. A touch of this sharpness of air and landscape makes me realize that the above may not sound so clear-cut. I really started out to tell you that I am trying hard to make it so for myself (and others).

PART 2

I just fished a note from my correspondence file with your name on it. It goes back twelve years to a period when I was out of work and doing all kinds of unremunerative things in the attempt to land on solid ground again. It was the time when you were having your show at Julien's (I had my first or second one just before or after) & circumstances link in the most curious manner the foregoing notes. The reason I meant to write to you (before this other) I because of the indelible impressions the sky-blue of your paintings left mingled with my canvassing experiences in strange out of the way parts (of Long Island & Brooklyn.) From all of that futile and endless wandering the actual places are blurred and romanticized. But a kind of essence seems to remain.

notation when sending letter – 'This' must have been the first ride as far as College Point village (not all the way as subsequently) when on a bitter cold day for bike riding the little butcher shop with its lone Jewish salesman evoked so graphically the world depicted by Chagall, its drabness and raw quality redeemed by a picturesqueness and touching humanity the girl waiting for the bus at the point where the delivery truck went by this letter as a 'raison d'être' for the FLORAL STILL-LIFE section

This letter shows distinctly their shared passion for the smallest observed detail and its pinning down, as in the 'enseigne', that sign the artist sees as a still-life, and as a meaningful sign in the universe for him to be inspired by in all its marvellous coincidence. That sense of the marvellous itself coincided with white magic, in which he so firmly believed, with the colours of his painterly vision, and with the force of the Christian Science he shared with Mina Loy. Cornell, who spent his days in old bookstores, cafés and antique shops, or under the trees in his backyard, felt a close companionship with the poet and painter and constructor who was his sister Scientist, and who was, like himself, always involved with the lunar and the celestial. What brought them together kept them together when they met and, when they didn't, in their own mental universe. Here he writes of such an experience:

> JULY 3, 1951
> Dear Mina,
> I had a beautiful early morning in the back yard under the Chinese quince tree – very early, in fact not much after five; and I could not help but think of you, looking up at the moon, when the first rays of the sun turn its gold into silver. A long time ago, you may remember, you told me that your destiny was ravelled up somehow with the lunar globe, but even aside from this I have always experienced something wonderful evoked in this mood.
> > Enclosed – a 'hot cross bum' item.
> > Con amore,

There is much to marvel at also in his looking at the moon and thinking of her and her lunar globe, especially this reference to her epic poem 'Hot Cross Bum'.

In a notebook entry of 8 May 1967, Cornell notes that he has been to see a painting by Mina at the Julien Levy Gallery; admiring her art, he went to see it as often as it was available, as she did with his boxes. Clearly, the particular affiliation of his *Aviary* with her own way of seeing and thinking was pertinent to much of their close friendship. Their friendship, in its unchallenged and innocent familiarity, was one of the firmest sustaining pillars of both their lives. For Mina Loy, Cornell was quite simply of the angelic order. And for him, she was as important a figure as the performers he celebrated over the ages.

7

NEW YORK AGAIN, 1936–53

Let me first claim both the British Mina Loy and the Romanian Tristan Tzara as desperately modern, and beyond both Dada and Surrealism. I am permitting myself that way-out claim first because of Mina Loy's ubiquitous and beautiful and strange presence, within Italian Futurism, not just as Marinetti's mistress, but as a remarkable advocate for the movement, as we see in her 'Aphorisms on Futurism' of 1914. Probably after unbecoming a Futurist, she substituted 'modern' for 'future' and 'modernism' for 'futurism' throughout the text, as Roger Conover points out.[1] So she might have preferred these to be 'Aphorisms on Modernism', but the title stands as she first had it. We can feel the influence of Marinetti, and this was preceded only by Flora Bonheur's *Diary of a Futurist Woman*, 1914, and can be seen as a riposte to Valentine de Saint-Point's 'Manifesto of the Futurist Woman' of 1912 and her 'Futurist Manifesto of Lust' of 1913. Loy's *Feminist Manifesto* of 1914 is a rough draft, but fascinating, as is her *Manifesto of Auto-Facial Construction*.

As for Tzara, my first Dada passion, persona non grata in his country because he was a Jew (born Sami Rosenstock), he exiled himself to Zurich, where he was the proto-Dada, then to Paris, where he was embroiled in all the Dada affairs, and then reunited with Breton as a Surrealist writer before his final total identification with the Communist party. In all his poetry we see the alternations of sun and shadow, motion and fixity, opposites and resolution, and imperfection or approximation.

I have put these two great poets together because their epic poems seem to me totally worth dwelling upon, and in, that is, dwelling Dadaistically. Tristan Tzara's great epic poem, *L'Homme approximatif* (The Approximate Man) of 1925–30, calls to me so strongly that I have translated it twice. I see it as a pilgrimage of language in nineteen cantos, a prolonged poetic journey in the 'groupings of interior order' as he feels them, towards a final freedom he calls poetry itself. My excerpts will be from the second translation, because Tzara, who wrote in Romanian before French, was as obsessed with words as Mina Loy, so we have the lists of vocabulary he wanted to use in the poem. I can simply point out how the idea of persons trying to make themselves as they go along, approximating themselves and something or other, seems to me relevant not just to existentialist thinking but to all of us now. *The Approximate Man* is big-deal epic stuff, with its remarkable and litanic ending close to T. S. Eliot's *The Waste Land*. It is interesting that the founder of Surrealism, André Breton, would pose the following question as an entrance test for those wanting to join that movement officially: 'Which are the greatest long poems of the twentieth century?' The answer was, as the playwright Arthur Adamov told me one evening here in New York: '*The Waste Land*, Guillaume Apollinaire's *Zone*, Breton's own *Ode to Charles Fourier*, of course, and Tzara's *L'Homme approximatif*.'

The Approximate Man, an ode to non-perfection, begins like some Baudelaire announcement about the animality of personhood and its sounding:

> sunday heavy lid on the seething of blood
>   fallen inside oneself found again
>   the bells ring for no reason and we too
>   we will rejoice at the clank of chains
>   that we will sound within us with the bells

The poem is constructed like a theme and variations, and is based on a series of recurring refrains:

> the bells ring for no reason and we too

and the second of the fifteen cantos begins again like an echo:

> the bells ring for no reason and we too
> we walk to escape the multiplying ways
> with a flask of scenery one illness only one
> one single illness that we nurture death
> I know I carry the tune in me and am not afraid
> I carry death and if I die it is death
> who will carry me in its imperceptible arms

The central refrain is already self-referential, language about language about our own being, approximate as it always is in its nature, and this is the theme of the entire epic poem:

> I think of the warmth spun by the word
> About this center the dream we call ourselves . . .

And the last canto concludes with an Eliotic refrain about another Waste Land announced in its harsh tones:

> and stony in my garments of schist I have pledged my waiting
>> to the torment of the oxidized desert
>> to the unshakable advent of fire

In the inevitable ending, I already hear Mina Loy's red-hot hellish and yet starry Bowery with its angelic bums, and see her wandering in her tattered robes, even as the poem enacts a reaching up through this wasted land to some higher place:

> harmony – let this word be banished from the feverish world I visit
> savage affinities undermined by emptiness covered with murders
> crying out at the impenetrable impasse sobbing with tattered flamingoes
> for the fire of anger varies the flickering of the subtle remains
> according to the mumbling modulations of hell
> that your heart strains to hear among the giddy salvos of stars
> and stony in my garments of schist
> I have pledged my waiting to the oxidized desert of torment
> to the unshakable advent of its flame[2]

There is of course no full stop and no ending to the waiting here: the pledge is like that.

Mina Loy, as beautiful as she was brainy, is a heroine of art for the ages. She wanted to make a foreign language, since English had already been used, parallel to Mallarmé's idea of rendering 'a purer sense to the words of the tribe' – thus her puns and neologisms. I won't deal with the famous, parodistic, long and excruciatingly complicated *Anglo-Mongrels and the Rose* of 1923–5, but instead the no less complicated but at once witty, distressing and bipolar 'Hot Cross Bum' of 1949.

Here, I need to point out something about place and these poems. Of course they are situated in the United States, in America, after Mina Loy's stays in England and Europe, and she would, in her time, become naturalized as American. But this poem is specifically about New York, where she lived from 1936 to 1953. During all the years Mina Loy lived there, before moving to Aspen to be with her daughters Joella and Fabi, she changed her residence many times, including stays on Lexington Avenue and East Thirteenth Street, East Sixty-Sixth Street and Second Street, and ended in the communal household of 5 Stanton Street near the Bowery. Fabi had lived with Irene Klemperer in the early 1940s, and that friend's mother ran a communal household, into which Mina Loy fitted perfectly.

It had the advantage, from the poetic point of view and less from the social one, of neighbouring on the Bowery. The poverty-stricken quarters had the advantage of inspiring one of Mina Loy's longest – in fact, epic – poems, 'Hot Cross Bum', which will be discussed in the interval chapter on how she looks, in both senses. There is often a sense of costuming, for Mina Loy generally dressed in dark-wine red, as if in some kind of priestly raiment. In Florence, as later, she had been noticed not just for her beauty but for her long skirts and elegant overgarments. Her clothes were always remarked on wherever she was, quite unlike the other inhabitants of the same realm, except in the Bowery, where in her nightgown she fitted in more properly.

'Hot Cross Bum' is preceded by a locally placed poem of 1942:

On Third Avenue
1.
'You should have disappeared years ago' —

so disappear
on Third Avenue
to share the heedless incognito

of shuffling shadow-bodies
animate with frustration

whose silence'   only potence is
respiration
preceding the eroded bronze contours
of their other aromas

through the monstrous air
of this red-lit thoroughfare.

Here and there
saturnine
neon-signs
set afire
a feature
on their hueless overcast
of down-cast countenances.

. . .

2.

Such are the compensations of poverty,
to see ─────────

. . .

Such are the compensations of poverty
to see ─────────

Transient in the dust,
the brilliancy
of a trolley
loaded with luminous busts;

lovely in anonymity
they vanish
with the mirage
of their passage.³

    This red-lit neon-signed opening of the space on Third Avenue will be disappearing into the Bowery, where Mina Loy was living at this point. It monstrously absorbs the gaunt bodies reduced to shadows of their former selves, and so indistinct from each other that they are incognito, anonymous and colourless, all in all, totally downcast in countenance and figure. Astonishingly, the trolley rushes by through the poverty and dust and waste, contrasting with the shuffling shadows, and so speedy is it that the faces within it do not register except as a mirage. And yet, they can see the passers-by, some bejewelled and glittery, and can see the dust spouting up as the trolley passes – such are the compensations of their pitiful lives.

There is also a poem from the 1940s about 14th Street:

Mass-Production on 14th Street

Ocean in flower
of closing hour

Pedestrian ocean
of whose undertow,
the rosy scissors of hosiery
snip space
to a triangular racing lace

in an iris circus of Industry.

As a commodious bee
the eye
gathers the infinite facets
of the unique unlikeness
of faces;
the diamond flesh of adolescence
sloping toward perception:

flower over flower,
corollas of complexion
craning from hanging-gardens
of the garment-worker.

All this Eros' produce
dressed in audacious

fuschia,
orgies of orchid
or dented dandelion
among a foliage of mass-production:

carnations
tossed at a carnal caravan
for Carnevale.
    Now
In the sedative descent of dusk
the street returns to stone.
Alone
Two lovers,
crushed together in sweet conjecture
as to Fashion's humour
point at the ecru and ivory
replica of the dress she has on
doused in a reservoir of ruby neon

Only – her buttons are clothespins:
the mannequin's,
harlequins.[4]

How wonderful to begin with 'now'. Mina Loy knew about presence, and knew how to celebrate it in major and minor ways. This view of the street – and we have become accustomed to her street views, of the nightclubs of London and Paris and Florence, and later of the Bowery with her 'Street Sisters' and her 'Hot Cross Bum' – adds to those street scenes, not in the daytime of the first or the afternoon (I am supposing this) of the second, but a twilight scene, all the more effective for its viewing of a couple. She, impoverished and wearing a replica of a replica, imitating the joy of fashion, is illuminated by the street lights, prefiguring the Bowery bum scene before the arrival of the churchly delivery. This is presence done fully in the fashion of the street as stage, and the poem as the delivery of its own message, the verbal replica of the vestimentary one.

Vision on Broadway

Seldom the accustomed heart
succumbs to sentiment
seldom an appearance
on the street
seldom a vision
attains perfection

(Maybe it was only a boy in uniform amused to array his baby son as his own replica that pedestrian and streetcar did not cheer or bow down before this American soldier)[5]

I do not take this indeed sentimental refusal of sentiment as ironic: it seems to me, now reading it, that this poem forms part of Mina Loy's real salute to America and the American dream, about which, as with much, she was of two minds. The triple repetition of the 'seldom' protects against anything at all sloppy – that, Mina never was – and this is just a single sighting of the uniform. I am placing it alongside her objects made during wartime, with flags and V for victory, and not only for commercial reasons, I think, but with some genuine affection and admiration for the military exercising itself ... and the replica here and in this other unpublished poem, perhaps from the same time period, says something about the repetition itself. It is in fact a quite moving poem, including its own metadata.

Still another poem is meant to be grouped with these, 'Chiffon Velours':

She is sere.

Her features
verging on a shriek
reviling age,

flee from death in odd directions
somehow retained by a web of wrinkles.

The site of vanished breasts
is marked by a safety pin.

Rigid,
at rest against the cornerstone
of a department store.

Hers alone to model
the last creation,

original design
of destitution.

Clothed in memorial scraps

skimpy even for a skeleton.

Trimmed with one sudden burst
of flowery cotton
half her black skirt
glows as a soiled mirror
reflections the gutter –
a yard of chiffon velours.[6]

These downcast figures will reappear in a singular fashion in an unfinished poem of the 1940s or '50s that will lead the way. 'I Almost Saw God in the Metro' salutes a figure who is quite other, a bum prefiguring Mina's angel Bowery Bums, for this 'animated coma' says it all, or almost: the tipsy knocked-out being who has about him an air of royalty, blooming amid the garbage and remaining royal. The Emperor of Void triumphs over, reigns over, the garbage.

I Almost Saw God in the Metro

In that state of animated coma
the condition of clochard
this gray-head slumped on a platform bench
like the Emperor of Void
on a throne to which no one pretends
is wrapped in aloofness august
as deity –
an inordinate flower
opening undefiled
among ordure.[7]

This poem seems complete, does not call for a further development, is its own statue unslumped, godlike indeed, and about to blossom right where it is, and it could be anywhere. The point is the figure's purity in its own emptiness of hope: this Void is our world, in the subway or out in the world.

This brings to our poetic memories Wallace Stevens's 'Emperor of Ice Cream', an unheroic statue, to all visible appearances, of a down-and-out figure who embodies the spiritual universe, just being a 'roller of big cigars, the muscular one', who is the ruler of all the universe, sweet and less so.

Let us gather into this same universe a contemporary poet who knows how to salute another poet, summoning Grace Schulman's poem about Auden in the metro:

Notes from Underground: W. H. Auden on the Lexington Avenue IRT

Hunched in a corner seat, I'd watch him pass
riders who gaped at headlines: '300 DEAD,'
and, in their prized indifference to all
others, were unaware he was one who heard
meter in that clamor of wheels on rails.

Some days I took the local because he did:
He sank down into plastic, his bruised sandals
no longer straining with the weight of him;
there, with the frankness of the unacquainted
I studied his face, a sycamore's bark

with lichen poking out of crevices.

> His eyes lifted over my tattered copy
> of his *Selected Poems*, then up to where
> they drilled new windows in the car and found,
> I guessed, tea roses and a healing fountain.
>
> All memories are echoes: some whisper,
> others roar, as this does. Dazed by war
> I, who winced at thunder, knew that train
> screeched 'DISASTER!' How it jolted and veered,
> station after station, chanting *Kyrie*
>
> *eleison*, while metal clanged on metal
> and bulbs went dim. Peering at tracks, I heard,
> 'Still persuade us to rejoice' I glimpsed
> a worn sandal, turned, and then my eyes
> met his eyes that rayed my underworld.[8]

There is nothing derogatory and everything celebratory in this truly glorious praise of sandals bruised and worn, and a tree-like face, a 'gray-head slumped' on the platform bench, like one of Mina Loy's angelic bums of the Bowery amid the garbage leavings and building wreckage and shards of bottles, blossoming undefiled forever on a throne that only poets can know how to salute, wherever such transfigured figures can be found, underground or on the streets, or somewhere else: the surrounding are in any case transcended. This is, again, Mina Loy's Christian Science vision, like that of Joseph Cornell.

8

ASPEN, 1953–66

At 71 years of age, Mina Loy was moved, by her daughters, from New York to Aspen, Colorado, in 1953. Fabi was divorced from Hans Frankel and married to the architect Fritz Benedict, while Joella was divorced from the handsome and philandering Julien Levy and married to Herbert Bayer, an Austrian artist trained at the Bauhaus, where he had also taught. There was a show about the Bauhaus in 2020 at the Cooper-Hewitt Museum in Manhattan, in which Bayer's constructions – rigid, said my daughter, like German, Austrian constructions – were displayed. His employer in Aspen, Walter Paepcke, head of the American Container Corporation, was restoring a bygone mining town in Colorado as a ski resort and an intellectual and cultural centre; eventually it became the world-famous Aspen Institute.

Here in Aspen arrived Mina Loy, with her long white hair, wearing noticeable clothing as always, yet unhappy about her so-changed appearance, to be near her two daughters. The one paved street in the town, deteriorated in status, was covered with snow, and the place had an empty feeling, with its nine hundred persons, after New York's teeming crowds. Paepcke, Herbert Bayer's friend of long standing, wanted to make it a centre 'for the whole man', which seemed to include artistry and athletics. Above all, there were to be 'great books, great men, and great music' — lots of persons around (we might notice, there was no call for any women to be around). And, from some points of view, Mina's outlook remained strong.

Indeed, Mina Loy had one of the most astoundingly open panoramas of a brain ever evolved, and I want to bring to our reading her poems on those topics, without needless and extraneous comment:

Evolution

Sun ray
shines on gelatinous cell
sets it aquiver

ensues a feeble agitation
in an ocean.

Since —
through aeons
life dons

increasingly
complex organisms
streamlined for survival

evolution's
exasperation of nervous systems
sharpens our wits,
expedites our improvement —

what, in infinitude,
will be our contour,
our density,
our potency?[1]

Mina Loy knew and cared about scientific discoveries, and much of her poetic vocabulary is related to that knowledge. A detectable excitement comes through in the words 'aquiver' and 'agitation', for it is clearly something she wanted to invite into her poems, this kind of sun ray shining. Take, for example, the 'Auto-facial construction' in which she believed,[2] and not only for its commercial potential (although it didn't work). The concept of evolution mattered to her greatly, as did theories concerning how our various organs became complexified and our brains more acute. She was also good at imagining the possible futures for humans and their abilities, and their shapes. I love the word 'infinitude' in the last stanza of the poem, and her general enlargement of all the person can reach out towards.

As for her brain and its memory – Arthur Cravan is never far from her mind and her memory is full of him, together with the enduring mystery of his disappearance – she would continue to write about them as in this poem.

Brain

Radio pulp
stacked
with microscopic
recordings

> drumming on time
> trivia of the past
>
> Automatic
> disc-server
> ceaselessly
> sabotaging
> my choice
> of selections
> lapsing
> my memory
> too fast[3]

All goes too quickly, for her (and for everyone), as did her time with Cravan. Even though they had no funds at all, not enough to nourish themselves, she looked back on it, including its trivia, as happy, for they were together. To what extent can the lover of the past control remembrance, even in its infinitude and its improvement?

It has to be said that Mina at this crucial time of her life did not feel up to the social scene. As she describes herself, so altered, in her late poem 'An Aged Woman':

> The past has come apart
> events are vaguing
> the future is inexploitable

the line in this poem expressing the moment directly after the terrible term 'inexploitable' is marked by a blank space before arriving at the emotion it produces:

the present   pain.

Does your mirror Bedevil you
or is the impossible
possible to senility
enabling the erstwhile agile
narrow silhouette of self –
to hold in huge reserve
this excessive incognito –
of a Bulbous stranger
only to be exorcised by death

Dilation has entirely eliminated
    Your long reality.
    Mina Loy
    July 12
        1984[4]

A newly grim self-portrait. The post-dating of the poem, as a premonition, is startling. Conover explains that at the time of composition, its dating uncertain but definitely late, the meeting of the self's encounter with the reflected image seems spectral indeed, and the situation of the poem itself is problematic, given the post-dating. 'An attempt, perhaps, to blur the lines between spatial, temporal and psychological modalities, and a teleology, if not a demonstration, of dementia's tricky logic.'[5] Mina Loy was not clear-headed in these last times, to be sure, and yet her poetry has an unshakable force, as witnessed in these two poems, dealing with finality, powerfully:

Mina Loy in Aspen, c. 1957, photograph by Jonathan Williams.

Breath Bank

Breath is the march of life.

If only civilians –
 waiting upon heroism –
could, to the mortuary of earth,
draw air from the populace's
 copious afflatus

in restitution for the fighter's breath
failing to come,
breathe from unbroken breasts
to span the omissive
ushering in of death.[6]

Among her unpublished poems kept at the Beinecke, this one is clearly about her fear of dementia, excerpts from her long poem as an elegy to herself and to her lover Arthur Cravan:

Letters of the Unliving

The present implies presence
thus
unauthorized by the present
these letters are left authorless –
have lost all origin
since the inscribing hand
lost life – – –

The hoarseness of the past
croaks
from creased leaves
covered with unwritten writing
since death's erasure
of the writer –
erased the lover

. . .
and agony

ends in an equal grave
with ecstasy.

An uneasy mist
rises from this calligraphy of recollection

your documented terror of dementia

This package of ago
creaks with the horror of echo
. . .
O leave me
my final illiteracy
of memory's languor.

my preference
to drift in lenient coma
an older Ophelia
on Lethe.[7]

What an amazing poem of desperate love and loss and the mythic (Ophelia, Lethe), the classical and timeless erasure and forgetfulness of life through its very writing. This seems to me the heartbreaking summit of Mina Loy's unquestionable poetic genius.

A while back, my husband and I went to Aspen to celebrate something or other, and it felt enormously unlike New York, the recent New York, unlike Mina's New York, of course, with everything more expensive by far, even in the Bowery, now gone. A week in Aspen seemed to me a century long, a vision of luxury and upscale living, taking into account the groceries, the over-the-top clothing and its prices, unbelievable, even from a New Yorker's point of view. It gave me a sense of how unusual Mina Loy must have looked, even back then, in her self-designed velvet frocks with the scarab jewellery. And her hemline dragging to the ground, as it always did, over her elegant shoes.

We must wonder how in the world she 'fitted' into the world of Aspen, which she did not. And did. Imagine her in the Hotel Jerome, now so overplushed with its incredibly small coffee rooms I had to visit, not in my velvet self-designed gowns, but as someone just caring about and writing about Mina Loy – of whom, let me say, the present owners seem not to have heard and about whom they couldn't have cared. Still, I was and am now caring a lot, determined to write even now, all these years later, on Mina Loy, because, now, 21 years after I was supposed to write this, I have learned to care about her, her past and her remarkable history.

Now in Aspen, where so many came to interview Mina Loy, Jonathan Williams and many others, she seemed to me to be, even years after I had been there, the entrance to a place in which – however I was garbed, and never with her elegance – I hope I might have known, like Mina Loy, how to be myself.

Interestingly, from all points of view, it was not only Aspen itself but the world of Mina Loy, and Aspen, and the cultural everything to which – even after many years – Mina Loy had given me an entrance, that I could now celebrate: the place to which Mina Loy moved, where she died on 25 September 1966, and was buried in a modest place to which I and many like me have paid homage, and where she was able to live as she chose to live, as a famous recluse.

Now she no longer had her gorgeous hair, for it was white. She no longer had her shining teeth, for they were gone. Was her 'beauty' gone? Never. She was never (as I read and somehow know) deprived of her beauty, not the real beauty. So let me say now, as a kind of postface, that finishing the present writing, I can say how important it is for me, the after-coming biographer of Mina Loy and an enthusiast of her art and poetry – how it turns out to be of major importance for me, my writing and my living – that she went right on, exclusive in herself, reclusive in herself, being herself. For she never really fitted in, not into Aspen's way of seeing or being. Even here, as she had been all her life – so attuned to the elements of decoration, from lamp-shades to hats to ritual costuming – she was, above all else, noticeable. She had always been remarked on for her clothes wherever she was. Her elegant robes of velvet and brocade and her turbans were outlandish, even as the streets were hard to walk on: cracked stones, mud. She wrote to Joseph Cornell, yet another reason for my feeling immensely close to her: 'I am not at my ease here but the altitude is stimulating – sometimes surprising. When I arrived, my hair stood on end and crackled with electricity, the metal utilities give electric shocks under one's fingernails – the radio is a volley of shots except at night – & in the streets mostly all there is to walk on are 3 cornered stones.'[8]

The Aspen Institute flourishes now, as it did from the time it was set up. Joella and Fabi were there and were always close to their mother. A great deal of refurbishing of the Hotel Jerome took place, where Mina had her grapefruit in the dining room. She would have taken her tea – although now American, she kept up that eternal habit at a café just over the way from the hotel, the Epicure. (Never did she stop smoking.) It was as infor-mal as the Jerome was formal, and even now serves tea and biscuits and ordinary fare. Mina loved it because it had a garden. At the Jerome she felt out of place, but would occasionally meet visitors there. First she lived in a small apartment, across the hall from Fritz and Fabi, above Fritz's office, and later (having felt too isolated in the Benedict's house on Red Mountain), her daughters moved her back to the same building as before, in a larger apartment there, with a light front room to be used as her studio and a bed-sitting room. Her scrap piles, with all the objects accumulated over her long lifetime, those 'suffering souls', could not be touched. They were, along with her daughters, her home, even as her mind was not always there. Fabi came to see her every day, and Joella often. She also had a companion for a few hours each day, Esther Jane Herwick, who, despite her fifteen years and Mina's 75, became a great friend. Esther would prepare wheatgerm dishes and puddings for Mina, as well as the horrendous mixture of ground raw liver mixed with grapefruit juice. Esther loved hearing about those suffering souls, and watching the tin cans and eggshells become a figure's clothing or part of the earth.

When Mina had finished work, she and Esther would have tea at the Epicure. By the late 1950s she no longer frequented the Epicure and stayed at home. Then Mrs Bibbig agreed to look after Mina, upstairs in her Victorian home. She returned there after a short stay in a nursing home, and later had a children's nurse in attendance. In 1966 she was hospitalized again, this time with spinal osteoarthritis.

Everywhere Mina Loy moved and went, and lived and roomed, those around her had to be extra-careful with all she accumulated. These objects were to be reused instead of being thrown away. (These were the 'suffering things', and the *objets/objects* refusés/refugees.) Everyone around her had to be careful with all the eggshells and other detritus out of which she made her constructions, of which many, from beginning to end, are decidedly peculiar. One has the odd face of that fisherman in *Christ on a Clothesline*, from the Bowery days.

Fortunately, as she would point out over and over, so much in her life is due to her good fortune and not just her talent, no, to luck, as she says, Christian Science assumes, as do we all. Jonathan Williams was in Aspen, and published, with his Jargon Press in 1958, her *Lunar Baedeker* and *Time-Tables*, with prefatory essays by William Carlos Williams, Kenneth Rexroth and Denise Levertov.

In 1958 in New York, an exhibition and party were held for her at the Martha Jackson Gallery, which she did not attend. However, she phoned many of her friends who went to the exhibition, and was always delighted to be on the phone with someone. In fact, her long-distance phone bills mounted very high, so in order to avoid those bills, Fabi would sometimes pretend to be a nearby Christian Science practitioner and give good counsel on the telephone. Her mother was delighted with the conversations, saying, 'They always seem to put you right.'[9]

In these last days, Mina Loy was recorded in an interview. Jonathan Williams, the Aspen Institute's Poet in Residence, and Paul Blackburn conducted it, Robert Creeley being indisposed. Paul and Robert Vas Dias, director of the Aspen Writers' Workshop, managed the interview. Mina Loy held forth on Stephen Haweis, a 'dwarf husband', and on the fun of being a bit wicked and mischievous in her poem recounting the erotic burrowing of 'Pig cupid' and all the snufflings in the poems about 'Joannes'.

Testimonials came in, one – much appreciated – from the monk and writer Thomas Merton, who especially liked the poems 'On Third Avenue' and 'Apology of Genius'. The latter, quoted again here, is understandably about his perception of her quite extraordinary life:

> We are the sacerdotal clowns
> who feed upon wind and stars
> and pulverous pastures of poverty
> . . .
> In the raw cavers of the Increate
> we forge the dusk of Chaos
> to that imperious jewelry of the Universe
>   – the Beautiful –
>
> While to your eyes
>   A delicate crop
> of criminal mystic immortelles
> stands to the censor's scythe.

He ended his letter with the welcome words: 'So may you be blessed and be at peace.'[10]

Plagued by pre-diabetes and osteoarthritis, Mina Loy, now edentate and mustachioed, nevertheless wrote about her visions, part of the Christian Science outlook she shared with her close friend Joseph Cornell. They had shared much, verbally, visually and in the life of objects: in 1946 she had written to Cornell of her gratitude for 'the indelible impression the sky-blue of your painting left mingled with my canvassing experiences in strange out-of-the-way parts' and remembered their conversations: 'I wish that all the details of your interesting conversation could stay with me as much as the spirit of it does.'[11]

Love Songs.

I.

Spawn of Fantasies
Silting the appraisable
Pig Cupid   his rosy snout
Rooting erotic garbage
"Once upon a time"
Pulls a weed   white star-topped
Among wild oats sown in mucous-membrane
I would   an eye in a Bengal light
Eternity in a sky-rocket
Constellations in an Ocean
Whose rivers run no fresher
Than a trickle of saliver

~~There are~~

These are suspect places

I must live in my lantern
Trimming subliminal flicker
Virginal   to the bellows
Of Experience

           Coloured glass

      Mina Loy.
      1915.

Mina Loy, 'Love Songs', 1915, autograph manuscript poem.

We are but a ramshackle edifice around an eternal exaltation, a building in which the moralities are a flight of stairs whose bases dissolve in the wake of our ascension . . . Being alive is a queer coincidence[12]

What I most love in looking back on this writing, and her magnificently complex work and odd life, is that many-faceted shape she bestowed upon them both, and now, in extension and immensity, us all.

9

ALWAYS AMPLE SPACE

Aspen is at the end of things, and provided a perfect ending for this poet and artist in all senses. On her move to Aspen, Mina Loy found herself awkward and old, with long white hair and no longer her delicate features and slim self, as she so painfully describes in her poem 'A Woman' –

> Does your mirror Bedevil you
> or is the impossible
> possible to senility
> enabling the erstwhile agile
> narrow silhouette of self
> to hold in huge reserve
> this excessive incognito
> of a Bulbous stranger
> only to be exorcised by death

This was the time to set off a

Time-Bomb

The   present   moment
is   an   explosion   ,
a   scission
of   past   and   future

leaving
those   valarous   disreputables   ,
the   ruins ,

sentinels
in   an   unknown   dawn
strewn   with   prophecy .

Only   the   momentary
goggle   of   death
fixes   the   fugitive
momentum   .¹

This poem of 1945 is not one of dementia, but rather of realization. It is not a late poem, although it was published in a late time in Mina Loy's life, between the covers of *Between Worlds*.² Yes, Mina Loy was always conscious of death, and, here in Aspen, of its near arrival.

Again, in the second stanza and all through, there are gaps between words, and punctuation. The poem gasps for breath. The last stanza ends with a final full stop, so that only the momentary goggle of death fixes the 'fugitive momentum' of the first three stanzas.

I want to take up the remark of Gilbert Neiman about Mina Loy not 'allowing herself the ample spaces' she once did, relating those spaces not only to this poem, but to her life and the way in which we aftercomers might perceive it. For one thing, this poem as it stands here, in its utterly bizarre and grand punctuation, is reminiscent of Gerard Manley Hopkins's innovations in his own poems, including the incredibly moving 'My Heart Let Me More Have Pity On', with its final joy (and I like to imagine Mina Loy's having a bit of that uncondescending pity also):

> . . . let joy size
> At God knows when to God knows what; whose smile
> 's not wrung, see you; unforeseen times rather – as skies
> Betweenpie mountains – lights a lovely mile.[3]

I am contemplating that large gap between the 'smile' and the 's' on the next line: how avant-garde of the great Hopkins.

The gaps, the ample space allowed the words, is my focus here in citing this so out-of-the-ordinary poem by the out-of-the-ordinary life of Mina Loy, in all its senses. I could also comment on her being some sort of mystical hermit, rather like Joseph Cornell's aviary, with its ample implication of a space beyond any cage. Mina Loy's spaces were ample beyond her Aspen days and others' perception of her partial dementia. She was deeply into Hopkins's call at the end of 'The Leaden Echo and the Golden Echo':

> We follow, now we follow. –
>   Yonder, yes yonder, yonder,
>   Yonder.[4]

I want to *not* finish with an undated poem, which should and will always hover in its lunar way over this text, as the *Lunar Baedeker*, *Lost* or *Last*, has guided us along. It takes no comment, for it says it all, whenever our poet wrote it.

Moreover, the Moon – – –

Face of the skies
preside
over our wonder.

Fluorescent
truant of heaven
draw us under.

Silver, circular corpse
your decease
infects us with unendurable ease,

touching nerve-terminals
to thermal icicles

Coercive as coma, frail as bloom
innuendoes of your inverse dawn
suffuse the self;
our every corpuscle become an elf.[5]

REFERENCES

Introduction: Why Mina Loy Now?

1 Carolyn Burke, *Becoming Modern: The Life of Mina Loy* (New York, 1996), p. 329.
2 Ibid., p. 238.
3 Ibid., pp. 264–5.
4 *Maintenant: Revue Littéraire* (October–November 1913), in Arthur Cravan, *Oeuvres: Poèmes, Articles, Lettres*, ed. Jean-Pierre Begot (Paris, 1987), pp. 49–63.
5 Rachel Potter and Suzanne Hobson, eds, *The Salt Companion to Mina Loy* (Cambridge, 2010), pp. 129, 133.
6 Tara Prescott, *Poetic Salvage: Reading Mina Loy* (Lewisburg, PA, 2017), p. xii.
7 Ibid., p. xxviii.
8 Fernando Pessoa, *The Book of Disquiet*, trans. Margaret Jull Costa, ed. Jerónimo Pizarro (New York, 2017); *The Complete Works of Alberto Caeiro*, trans. Margaret Jull Costa and Patricio Ferrari, ed. Jerónimo Pizarro and Patricio Ferrari (New York, 2020).

1 London and Munich, 1882–1900

1 Mina Loy, *The Last Lunar Baedeker*, ed. Roger L. Conover (Jargon Society: Highlands, NC, 1982; Carcanet Press: Manchester, 1985), p. 121.
2 Ibid., p. 124.
3 Ibid., pp. 143–4.
4 Carolyn Burke, *Becoming Modern: The Life of Mina Loy* (New York, 1996), p. 23.

5 Ibid., p. 43.
6 Ibid., p. 40.

2 'Parturition': Paris, Florence, New York, 1900–1916

1 Mina Loy, *The Lost Lunar Baedeker: Poems*, ed. Roger L. Conover (New York, 1996), pp. 67–71.
2 Ibid., pp. 130–32.
3 Tim Armstrong, 'Loy and Cornell: Christian Science and the Destruction of the World', in *The Salt Companion to Mina Loy*, ed. Rachel Potter and Suzanne Hobson (Cambridge, 2010), pp. 169–99.
4 Carolyn Burke, *Becoming Modern: The Life of Mina Loy* (New York, 1996), p. 111.
5 Ibid., p. 118.
6 Ibid., p. 135.
7 Loy, *The Lost Lunar Baedeker*, p. 238.
8 Among the unfinished manuscripts by Mina Loy held at the Beinecke Library, Yale University, New Haven, Connecticut. *Vide* Jonathan Williams's adaptation, 'Ripostes to Two Passages from Mina Loy's "Songge Byrd"', *Aspen*, 25 (1968), p. 327.

Interval: Futurism

1 Filippo Tommaso Marinetti, *Selected Writings*, ed. R. W. Flint (New York, 1971), pp. 3–4.
2 Ibid., p. 12.
3 Ibid., p. 18.
4 Ibid., p. 6.
5 Ibid., p. 30. Citation from Walter Benjamin, 'The Work of Art in the Age of Mechanical Reproduction', in *Illuminations*, trans. Harry Zorn (New York, 1969).
6 Jane Rye, *Futurism* (London, 1972), p. 115.
7 All the quotations come from papers in the Beinecke Rare Book and Manuscript Library at Yale University, New Haven, and from Roger Conover's notes in Mina Loy, *The Lost Lunar Baedeker: Poems*, ed. Roger L. Conover (New York, 1996), pp. 100 and 179.
8 Carolyn Burke, *Becoming Modern: The Life of Mina Loy* (New York, 1996), p. 188.

9 Ibid., p. 192.
10 Marinetti, *Selected Writings*, p. 21.
11 Ibid., p. 22.
12 Ibid., p. 23.
13 Ibid., p. 16.
14 Filippo Tommaso Marinetti, 'The Founding and Manifesto of Futurism', in *Futurist Manifestos*, ed. Umbro Apollonio (New York, 1973), pp. 19–23. This is from the first page, p. 19.
15 Ibid., p. 23.
16 Ibid., pp. 70–73.
17 Ibid., pp. 95–106.
18 Ibid., pp. 154–9.
19 Ibid., pp. 12–13.
20 Marinetti, *Selected Writings*, p. 5.
21 Rye, Futurism, p. 37.
22 Ardegno Soffici in Marinetti, *Selected Writings*, p. 55.
23 Ibid., p. 34.
24 Hart Crane, 'To Brooklyn Bridge' [1933], from *The Complete Poems of Hart Crane*, ed. Marc Simon (New York, 1986), pp. 43–4.
25 Loy, *The Lost Lunar Baedeker*, p. 178.
26 Ibid., p. 15.
27 Loy, *The Lost Lunar Baedeker*, pp. 16–17.
28 Ibid., pp. 19–20.
29 Ibid., pp. 27–32.
30 Loy, *The Last Lunar Baedeker*, p. lxix.
31 Loy, *The Lost Lunar Baedeker*, p. 197.
32 Mina Loy to Carl Van Vechten, 1914, Carl Van Vechten papers, Beinecke Rare Book and Manuscript Library, Yale University, New Haven.
33 Loy, *The Lost Lunar Baedeker*, pp. 46–50.
34 Ibid., pp. 36–9.
35 Ibid., p. 221.

3 Diversions, 1914–53

1 Sara Crangle, ed., *Stories and Essays of Mina Loy* (Champaign, IL, Dublin and London, 2011).
2 Ibid., p. 25.

3 Ibid., pp. 65, 96.
4 Ibid., p. 141.
5 Ibid., pp. 104–8.
6 Ibid., pp. 230–31.
7 Ibid., pp. 290–93.
8 Ibid., pp. 237–52.

4 New York and the Arensberg Circle

1 'Songs to Joannes', in Mina Loy, *The Lost Lunar Baedeker: Poems*, ed. Roger L. Conover (New York, 1996), p. 53.
2 Carolyn Burke, *Becoming Modern: The Life of Mina Loy* (New York, 1996), p. 196.
3 Mina Loy, *The Last Lunar Baedeker*, ed. Roger L. Conover (Manchester, 1985), p. 285.
4 'She broke every rule on the page, made up her own grammar, invented her own work – even improvised her own punctuation.' Conover in *The Lost Lunar Baedeker*, p. xv.
5 Ibid., p. xiii.
6 Charles Nicholl on the disappearance of Arthur Cravan in the *London Review of Books*, 'Diverted Traffic: A New Almost-Daily Newsletter from the LRB', 18 March 2020.
7 In this 'verbal collage' or spoof on the social life of Greenwich Village Louise is Louise Arensberg; it was published in the second and final number of *The Blind Man* (May 1917), ed. Marcel Duchamp, Henri-Pierre Roché and Beatrice Wood.
8 Francis M. Naumann, *New York Dada: The Arensberg Circle of Artists* (New York, 2019), p. 1.
9 Burke, *Becoming Modern*, p. 186.
10 Walter Conrad Arensberg, 'To a Poet', in *Poems* (New York, 1914).
11 Often, often: see my *Creative Gatherings: Meeting Places of Modernism* (London, 2019), with a plenitude of circles and gossip.
12 Naumann, *Dada*, p. 14.
13 Ibid., p. 24.
14 All these details, salacious and otherwise, are referred to in a note on p. 14 of Naumann, *Dada*: 'It should be acknowledged that a certain degree of poetic licence was taken in composing the foregoing narrative, for some of the events that are described could

not have taken place on the date assigned for the scene, May 25, 1917, the evening of the Blindman's Ball . . . It is also unlikely that Arthur Cravan was at the Arensbergs on this particular evening, as he and Mina Loy would have spent the night together (instead of her retiring to Duchamp's studio). There is also no evidence that Baroness Elsa attended this party – or, for that matter, any others at the Arensberg apartment – as she was then living in Philadelphia.' What Naumann presents here he calls 'more an amalgam of the sort of evening you might have encountered at the Arensbergs in this general period through to the time of Duchamp's departure for Buenos Aires in 1918, when these legendary informal gatherings were a near-nightly occurrence.'

15 From Robert McAlmon, *Being Geniuses Together* (New York, 1938), p. 41, quoted in Virginia Kouidis, *Mina Loy: American Modernist Poet* (Baton Rouge, LA, 1980), p. 105.

Interval: Arthur Cravan

1 Arthur Cravan, *Oeuvres: Poèmes, Articles, Lettres*, ed. Jean-Pierre Begot (Paris, 1987).
2 In the *London Review of Books*, 'Diverted Traffic: A Newish Almost-Daily Newsletter from the LRB', 18 March 2020. Here we read Charles Nicholl on the disappearance of Arthur Cravan. I think it portentous of the interest we might now pay to Cravan that this appears as the very first Diverted Traffic: not that he is diverting, but that, when you read about him, you feel it was worth being diverted, whatever you might have been trafficking in.
3 Félix Fénéon, Archinard's dealer and Cravan's friend, had paintings shown in the pages of Emmanuel Guignon's *Arthur Cravan: Maintenant?* (Barcelona, 2017), pp. 87–99, in the article by Jean-Paul Morel, 'Archinard, una mistificafion', about which there is nothing but mystery indeed. The article is on pp. 65–101.
4 Willard Bohn, 'Chasing Butterflies with Arthur Cravan', *Dada/Surrealism*, 14 (1985), pp. 120–23.
5 Ibid., p. 120.
6 Ibid., p. 121.
7 *4 Dada Suicides: Arthur Cravan, Jacques Rigaut, Julien Torma, Jacques Vaché* (London, 2005), p. 23.

8 Roger L. Conover's piece in *Dada/Surrealism*, 'Mina Loy's "Colossus": Arthur Cravan Undressed', 14 (1985), pp. 102–19, with its excerpts from Mina's *Colossus*, is invaluable. First, for its information, difficult to locate otherwise, but also, and principally, for this major source of the remembrance of the far larger-than-life Cravan, already pretty large.
9 Ibid., p. 119.
10 Roger Conover's notes in *The Last Lunar Baedeker* (Highlands, NC, 1982), p. xlvii.
11 Conover, 'Mina Loy's "Colossus": Arthur Cravan Undressed'.
12 *4 Dada Suicides*, p. 23.
13 Ibid., p. 31.
14 Ibid., p. 32.
15 Eric C. Losfeld, *Maintenant* (Paris, 1957), p. 51.
16 Terry Hale's translation of Arthur Cravan's notes from *Maintenant*, from Mary Ann Caws, ed., *Surrealist Painters and Poets: An Anthology* (Boston, MA, 2001), pp. 169–73.
17 All material from Guignon, *Arthur Cravan*.
18 Ibid., p. 266.
19 Ibid., p. 214.
20 The translations of Cravan's texts are by Terry Hale: 'To Be or Not To Be American', and the notes are by Terry Hale; the translation of 'Whistle' is my own.
21 Ibid., p. 267.
22 Ibid., p. 305.
23 Eric Weiss, 'Post-Scriptum', ibid., pp. 305–11.
24 Rachel Potter and Suzanne Hobson, eds, *The Salt Companion to Mina Loy* (Cambridge, 2010), p. 167.
25 A full biography to be referred to is that of Maria Lluisa Borràs, *Arthur Cravan: Una biografia* (Barcelona, 1993).
26 Ibid., p. 274.
27 Ibid., p. 276.
28 Cravan, *Oeuvres*, p. 232: 'Marcel Duchamp – "Je le connaissais bien et seule la mort a pu être cause de sa disparition. New York, 2 mars 1946." Henri Robert Marcel Duchamp (attestation recueillie sous la foi du serment ce deuxième jour de mars 1946, Max M. Livite, notaire, comté de New York).' (I attest to this statement under oath, Max M. Livite, notary public, New York).

5 'The Widow's Jazz': Paris Again

1 Carolyn Burke, *Becoming Modern: The Life of Mina Loy* (New York, 1996), p. 341.
2 As Burke says, most of these unattributed quotations come from the correspondence between Mina Loy and her daughters.
3 Mina Loy, *The Lost Lunar Baedeker: Poems*, ed. Roger L. Conover (New York, 1996), pp. 95–7.
4 Mina Loy, *The Last Lunar Baedeker*, ed. Roger L. Conover (Highlands, NC, 1982), p. 27.
5 Harriet Monroe, 'The Editor in France', *Poetry*, XXIII (1923), pp. 95–6. From Virginia M. Kouidis, *Mina Loy: American Modernist Poet* (Baton Rouge, LA, 1980), p. 12.

6 Insel, 1933–6

1 Mina Loy, *Insel (Neversink)*, ed. and afterword by Elizabeth Arnold (Santa Rosa, CA, 1991), reprinted with an introduction by Sarah Hayden (New York and London, 2014). Based on 'Visitation', material in the Beinecke Rare Book and Manuscript Library, New Haven, Connecticut.
2 It is a more than peculiar morsel and, from my point of view, totally indigestible.
3 Loy, *Insel*, p. 19.
4 Ibid., p. 22.
5 Ibid., p. 24.
6 Ibid., p 21.
7 Ibid., p. 37.
8 Ibid., p. 38.
9 Ibid., p. 43.
10 Ibid., p. 50.
11 Ibid., p. 93.
12 Ibid., p. 87.
13 Ibid., p. 175.
14 Ibid., p. 177. We are at least glad to have the mention of *Colossus*, the volume Mina Loy was writing about Cravan. Once again, everything in her life and writing seems to refer to much else.

15 Ibid., p. 179.
16 David Ayers, 'Mina Loy's Insel and Its Contexts', in *The Salt Companion to Mina Loy*, ed. Rachel Potter and Suzanne Hobson (Cambridge, 2010), pp. 221–47.
17 Ibid., pp. 221, 226.

Interval: Mina Loy the Artist

1 This material on the Provincetown Players is heavily dependent on Carolyn Burke, *Becoming Modern: The Life of Mina Loy* (New York, 1996), pp. 220–23.
2 See ibid., in particular pp. 186–9.
3 Mina Loy, *The Lost Lunar Baedeker: Poems*, ed. Roger L. Conover (New York, 1996), pp. 79–80.
4 Mina Loy, *The Last Lunar Baedeker*, ed. Roger L. Conover (Highlands, NC, 1982), pp. 133–44.
5 Burke, *Becoming Modern*, p. 405.

7 New York Again, 1936–53

1 Never mind that she would have preferred, as Roger Conover points out, the term 'modernism' to 'futurism' – the text stands as it is.
2 Tristan Tzara, *Approximate Man and Other Writings*, trans. Mary Ann Caws (Boston, MA, 2004), p. 12.
3 Mina Loy, *The Last Lunar Baedeker*, ed. Roger L. Conover (Highlands, NC, 1982), pp. 181–3.
4 Ibid., p. 246.
5 Ibid., p. 247.
6 Note by Roger Conover. This poem is found at the Beinecke Rare Books and Manuscripts Library at Yale, in the same folder as 'On Third Avenue' and 'Mass-Production on 14th Street'. Conover points out the details behind all the poems, writing about this period: 'She had once been a model and modiste; now she wore her nightgown in the street, part of the human shuffle known as the Bowery sidewalk ... now an insider in a world of outsiders ... When she scavenged the back alleys for flattened cans and abandoned mopheads it was not to fashion a shelter but to create

a poignant vision of shelterless existence.' Mina Loy, *The Lost Lunar Baedeker*, ed. Roger L. Conover (New York, 1996), p. 207.
7 Ibid., p. 248.
8 Grace Schulman, *Days of Wonder: New and Selected Poems* (Boston, MA, 2015), p. 83.

8 Aspen, 1953–66

1 Mina Loy, *The Last Lunar Baedeker*, ed. Roger L. Conover (Highlands, NC, 1982), p. 256.
2 Printed under the heading 'Didactic, Polemical and Prescriptive Writings', ibid., p. 283, it appeared as an advertisement in 1919 in Florence. Writing to Mabel Dodge on February 1920, and enclosing the brochure, Mina Loy said, 'I am enclosing a prospectus or a new method I shall teach when not drawing or writing about art. It came as a most unexpected revelation – & it works! I think the life-force inspired me with it – to solve the problem of keeping bodies alive without prostituting art.' Explanation by Conover, p. 328.
3 Loy, *The Last Lunar Baedeker*, pp. 282–3.
4 Late poem titled 'An Aged Woman', in the Beinecke Library ICAL, note by Roger Conover.
5 Mina Loy, *The Lost Lunar Baedeker: Poems*, ed. Roger L. Conover (New York, 1996), pp. 214–15.
6 'Breath Bank', from Loy, *The Last Lunar Baedeker*, p. 254.
7 'Lethe', ibid., p. 262.
8 Carolyn Burke, *Becoming Modern: The Life of Mina Loy* (New York, 1996), p. 427.
9 Ibid., p. 237.
10 Ibid., p. 439.
11 Mary Ann Caws, *Joseph Cornell: Theatre of the Mind: Diaries, Letters, Source Files* (London and New York, 1993), pp. 135–6.
12 Burke, *Becoming Modern*, p. 440.

9 Always Ample Space

1 The present text follows that version, identical to a signed typescript labelled 'Selection sent to "Between Worlds"', 1960, Mina Loy Papers: YCAL MSS 6.

Roger Conover points out that 'it is possible that Gilbert Neiman influenced the extra spaces between words and punctuation in this poem, for upon receiving the first batch of submissions from Mina Loy he wrote: 'For my part . . . you are not allowing yourself the ample spaces you once did' and continues that these were not the allowances he was referring to. In Mina Loy, *The Lost Lunar Baedeker: Poems*, ed. Roger L. Conover (New York, 1996), p. 212.
2   *Between Worlds*, 1/2 (Spring/Summer 1961), p. 200.
3   *Gerard Manley Hopkins: Poems and Prose*, ed. W. H. Gardner (Harmondsworth, 1957), p. 63.
4   Ibid., p. 54.
5   Loy, *The Lost Lunar Baedeker*, p. 146. Composition date unknown, based on the manuscripts at the Beinecke. This cannot help but remind us, in its way of completing the incomplete, and its undated form, of T. S. Eliot's *The Waste Land*, as it ends 'not with a bang but a whimper'. Not a bad ending.

SELECT BIBLIOGRAPHY

Adams, Bronte, and Trudi Tate, ed., *That Kind of Woman: Stories from the Left Bank and Beyond* (London, 1991)

Apollonio, Umbro, *Futurist Manifestos* (London, 1973)

The Blind Man, 2 (May 1917) (repr. New York, 2017)

Borràs, Maria Luisa, *Arthur Cravan: Una Biogragrafia* (Barcelona, 1993)

Burke, Carolyn, *Becoming Modern: The Life of Mina Loy* (New York, 1996).

Caws, Mary Ann, *Joseph Cornell's Theater of the Mind* (New York and London, 1993)

—, ed., *Dada/Surrealism*, 14 (1985)

—, ed., *Surrealist Painters and Poets: An Anthology* (Boston, MA, 2001)

Conover, Roger, 'Mina Loy's "Colossus": Arthur Cravan Undressed', with valuable excerpts from Mina Loy's "Colossus"', *Dada/Surrealism*, 14 (1985), pp. 102–19

Crangle, Sara, ed., *Stories and Essays of Mina Loy* (Champaign, IL, Dublin and London, 2011)

Cravan, Arthur, *Oeuvres: Poèmes, Articles, Lettres*, ed. Jean-Pierre Begot (Paris, 1987)

Elkins, Amy E., 'From the Gutter to the Gallery: Berenice Abbott Photographs Mina Loy's Assemblages', PMLA, CXXXIV/5 (2019), pp. 1094–103

Guignon, Emmanuel, ed., *Arthur Cravan: Maintenant?* (texts by Laurence Madeline, Jean-Paul Morel, Aitor Qjuiney, Georges Sebbag and Erich Weiss) (Barcelona, 2017)

Kouidis, Virginia M., *Mina Loy: American Modernist Poet* (Baton Rouge, LA, 1980)

Loy, Mina, *Insel* (Neversink), ed. and afterword by Elizabeth Arnold (Santa Rosa, CA, 1991), reprinted with an introduction by Sarah

Hayden (New York and London, 2014)
——, *The Last Lunar Baedeker*, ed. Roger L. Conover (Highlands, NC, 1982)
——, *The Lost Lunar Baedeker: Poems*, selected and edited by Roger L. Conover (New York, 1996)
——, *Stories and Essays of Mina Loy* (New York, 2011)
McAlmon, Robert, *Being Geniuses Together* (London, 1938)
Marinetti, Filippo Tommaso, *Selected Writings*, ed. R. W. Flint (New York, 1971)
Naumann, Francis, *New York Dada: The Arensberg Circle of Artists* (New York, 2019)
Potter, Rachel, and Suzanne Hobson, eds, *The Salt Companion to Mina Loy* (Cambridge, 2010)
Prescott, Tara, *Poetic Salvage: Reading Mina Loy* (Lewisburg, PA, 2017)
Schreiber, Maeera, and Keith Tuma, eds, *Mina Loy: Woman and Poet* (Orono, ME, 1996)
Steegmuller, Francis, ed., *'Your Isadora': The Love Story of Isadora Duncan and Gordon Craig* (New York, 1974)

ACKNOWLEDGEMENTS

First of all, how to express, still understating it, how essential the publications and permissions and guidance of Roger Lloyd Conover, my wise former editor at the MIT Press, have been to every stage of this project? I felt summoned when, on 11 March 1991, he bestowed on me a now rare copy of Mina Loy's *Last Lunar Baedeker*, saying I inhabited her same planetarium.

To the Beinecke Rare Book Library, where the staff has been wonderfully helpful over the years, I have had the privilege of using their resources, and to which I am giving all the precious letters and documents I have received from poets and artists, my warmest gratitude. To the Research Library team at the New York Public Library, and in particular to Melanie Locay, my manifold thanks for sending me home with two books by and about Arthur Cravan – without which I couldn't possibly have tackled the topic, no matter how much I had read previously. Like Mina herself, I fell repeatedly in love with that far larger-than-life being and personality, in New York and Rome and Paris.

Francis Naumann welcomed me into his gallery and shared his publications about the Arensberg circle, important to the background of this book. My students and friends at the Graduate School of the City University of New York, in the several PhD programmes they and I have inhabited over time, have shared my enthusiasm for Mina Loy, and I am delighted to thank Margo and Anthony Viscusi and Lee Briccetti of Poets' House for inviting me to chat about Mina Loy and Tristan Tzara's epic poems and personalities. Grace Schulman and I have been able to discuss poetry over the years, and Carolyn Burke's masterful book on Mina Loy was the wall against which this publication heavily and happily leans.

My really zippy longtime publisher, Michael Leaman, and his more than able assistant, Alexandru Ciobanu, and Martha Jay, my editor over a wonderfully long period, produced this volume in its long haul. I earnestly believe my daughter, Hilary Caws-Elwitt, never met a problem she couldn't solve, and this time it was the chaos of my enthusiasm for the subject that she managed to mould into one document. The encouragement of my son, the musician Matthew Caws of Nada Surf, and my husband, Dr Boyce Bennett, were crucial to this remarkably enduring project. How glad I am that much of Mina Loy's work was never finished, for which we can unendingly salute her.

PHOTO ACKNOWLEDGEMENTS

The author and publishers wish to express their thanks to the below sources of illustrative material and/or permission to reproduce it. Every effort has been made to contact copyright holders; should there be any we have been unable to reach or to whom inaccurate acknowledgements have been made please contact the publishers, and full adjustments will be made to any subsequent printings.

All artworks by Mina Loy – © 2021 The Estate of Mina Loy

Beinecke Rare Book and Manuscript Library, Yale University, New Haven, CT: pp. 55 (YCAL MSS 196), 64 (YCAL MSS 77), 135 and 140 (YCAL MSS 778), 193 (YCAL MSS 1050); collection of Carolyn Burke: p. 155; photos courtesy Roger Conover: pp. 6, 11, 19, 23, 29, 31, 32, 87, 111, 114, 119, 121, 141 (left), 185; photo DEA/G. Cigolini/De Agostini via Getty Images: p. 42; photos courtesy Fondazione Echaurren Salaris, Rome: pp. 36, 39; photos courtesy Galerie 1900-2000, Paris: pp. 8, 90, 103; George Grantham Bain Collection, Library of Congress, Prints and Photographs Division, Washington, DC: p. 81; © The Joseph and Robert Cornell Memorial Foundation/VAGA at ARS, NY and DACS, London 2021, photo courtesy Beinecke Rare Book and Manuscript Library, Yale University, New Haven, CT: pp. 151 (YCAL MSS 778); © Lee Miller Archives, England 2021 (all rights reserved), photo © 2021 The Art Institute of Chicago/Art Resource, NY/Scala, Florence: p. 143; © Man Ray 2015 Trust/DACS, London 2021, photo courtesy Department of Special Collections, Princeton University Library, NJ: p. 118; © Man Ray 2015 Trust/DACS, London 2021, photo courtesy Roger Conover: p. 146; collection of Francis M. Naumann and Marie T. Keller, Yorktown

Heights, NY: pp. 82–3 (reproduced with permission of Michel Vigourt), 132 (top) and 147 (photos courtesy Roger Conover), 152, 154; private collection: p. 94; private collection, photos courtesy Roger Conover: pp. 22, 26, 27, 99, 132 (bottom), 133, 136, 137, 141 (right); photo George Rinhart/Corbis via Getty Images: p. 139; courtesy The Rosenbach Museum & Library, Philadelphia, PA: p. 145; © Succession Brancusi (all rights reserved)/ADAGP, Paris and DACS, London 2021, photo courtesy Kasmin Gallery, New York: p. 149; © Succession Brancusi (all rights reserved)/ADAGP, Paris and DACS, London 2021, photo © 2021 The Metropolitan Museum of Art, New York/Art Resource, NY/Scala, Florence: p. 160.

INDEX OF WORKS BY MINA LOY

Visual

L'Amour dorloté par les belles dames 136
Bums Praying 155
Calla Lily lamp 140
Christ on a Clothesline 152, 154
Communal Cot 154
Dawn 132
Fallen Angels 133
Fashion Designs 26
Love Caressed by the Lovely Ladies 131
Man Ray 147
Mappamundo 135
Marianne Moore 145
Self-Portrait 137
Surreal Scene 27
Teasing a Butterfly 131, 132

Verbal

NOVELLA

Insel 122–30

PLAYS AND PARODIES

Collision 44
Cittapapini 44
The Gate Crashers of Olympus 70

The Pamperers 69–70
The Sacred Prostitute 69–70

POEMS

'An Aged Woman' 183–4
Anglo-Mongrels and the Rose 14–16, 148
'Apology of Genius' 192
'Brain' 182–3
'Brancusi's Golden Bird' 148–53
'Breath Bank' 185–6
'Café du Néant' 51
'Chiffon Velours' 176–7
'Evolution' 181–2
'Giovanni Franchi' 56
'Hot Cross Bum' 130, 148, 153–9, 165, 170, 177
'I Almost Saw God in the Metro' 177
'Letters of the Unliving' 186–7
'Lions' Jaws' 57–60
'Love Songs' 193
'Mass Production on 14th Street' 173–4
'Moreover, the Moon' 198
'On Third Avenue' 171–2
'One O'Clock at Night' 49
'Parturition' 24
'Prototype' 61
'Sketch of a Man on a Platform' 53, 88
'Songge Byrd (for Isadora Duncan)' 34
'Songs for Joannes' 76
'The Widow's Jazz' 112–18
'There Is Neither Life Nor Death' 120
'Three Moments in Paris' 49
'Time-Bomb' 196
'Vision on Broadway' 175
'A Woman' 195

STATEMENTS AND TREATISES, COMPLETE AND INCOMPLETE

'Aphorisms of Futurism' ('of Modernism') 76
'Colossus' 100–102
'Dialogue between Mi and Lo' 72–3
'The History of Religion and Eros' 74
'O Marcel' 79
'The Public and the Artist' 78

STORIES

'The Effectual Marriage; or, The Insipid Narrative of Gina and Miovanni' 60–61
'Gloria Gamma' 63
'Pazarella' 56
'The Stomach' 68
'Transfiguration' 67

GENERAL INDEX

Page numbers in *italics* indicate illustrations

Abbott, Berenice *149*
abstract 7
Académie Colarossi 7, 21
Adamov, Arthur 167
Albert-Birot, Pierre 102
America, Americanism 48, 102, 105, 175
Anderson, Margaret 148, *149*
Anglo-American 64
Anglo-Mongrels and the Rose 14, 18, 28, 170
antisemitism 14
Apollinaire, Guillaume 47, 87, 107, 145
Apollonio, Umbro 47
Arcetri 8, 64
Arensbergs (Walter, Louise) 8, 69, 76, 84–6, 89, 100, 104, 145
  Circle 82, 84
  Walter as a poet 84
Argentina 9, 110, 112
Ariadne 112
Armory Show 8, 63
Arnold, Elizabeth 122, *130*
Aspen 10, 180–94
Aspen Writers' Workshop 191
Auden, W. H. 178

Australia 33
avant-garde 71
  Les Aventures de Lafcadio 110
Ayers, David 129

Barcelona 110
Barney, Natalie 8, 70, 117
  Académie des femmes 117
Barnum, P. T. 38
Barnes, Djuna 117, *118*
  Ladies Almanack 117
Basilica de Guadalupe 110
Baudelaire, Charles 167
Bayer, Herbert 180, 190
Bayer, Joella 7, 10, 32, 115–16, *114*, 190
Beach, Sylvia 115
  Shakespeare & Company 115
  'the Crowd' 115
Beardsley, Aubrey 134
Beinecke Library 10, 63, 122, 186
Bell, Quentin 17
Benedict, Fabienne *114*, 170, 180, 190
  photograph of Arthur Cravan in Paris *103*
Benedict, Fritz 180, 190

General Index

Benjamin, Walter 180
Bergson, Henri 47, 65
Beuys, Joseph 112
Blackburn, Paul 191
Blind Man: A Magazine of Verse
 Art 84–8
Blindman's Ball 9, 84, 85, 138, 141, 147
Boccioni, Umberto 43, 47
Bohn, Willard 92
Bon Marché 128
Bowdoin College 11
Brancusi, Constantin 148, 149
 Bird in Space 160
Braque, Georges 70–71
Brazil 93
Breton, André 109, 112, 167
 Anthology of Black Humor 112
 Ode to Charles Fourier 167
Brooklyn 164
Bryan, Julia 14, 16, 18
Buenos Aires 9, 92, 100
Buffet, Gabrielle 88
Burden, Chris 112
Burke, Carolyn 16, 18, 73

Café de la Régence 109
Café du Neant 51
Caffè Giubbe Rosse 33, 43
Camera Work 88
Campagne Première, rue de 115
Cangiullo, Francesco 48
Capoulard Café 128
Capricorn 162
Carrà, Carlo 43
Carrière, Eugène 22
Carroll, Lewis 130
Catholicism 41

Cavell, Stanley 29
 Les Caves du Vatican 110
Cendrars, Blaise 94
Chagall, Marc 164
Christ 41, 62, 73, 161, 191
Christian Science 10, 13, 49, 116, 118, 162, 179, 191–2
Christianity 14
Coles, Henry 22
Colette 22
Colisée, rue de 116
College Point 164
Colossus ('mystic Colossus' = Cravan) 100–102
'Compensations of Poverty' 57
Conover, Roger Lloyd 184 and passim
Cornell, Joseph 13, 49, 79, 128, 151, 162, 163, 179, 192
Costa San Giorgio 33, 54
Cosway, Virginia 69
Craig, Gordon 31
Crane, Hart 48, 49
Crangle, Sara 63
Cravan, Arthur (Fabian Avenarius Lloyd) (Colossus) 8, 11, 12, 49, 67, 76–92, 80, 99, 103, 111, 117, 120, 127, 182–6
 'NOTES' to Maintenant 105
 'Le rythme de l'Océan...' 96
 Sculpture in a Park 90
 watercolour 94
Creely, Robert 191
Crèmerie Rosalie 115
Crowley, Alastair 130
Crystal Luc 117
Cubism 70–71
Cubo-Futurism 47–62

Dada 10, 47, 76, 86, 92, 120
D'Annunzio, Gabriele 37, 38, 48, 54, 56, 57–60
Dante Alighieri 41
Dasio, Maximilian 20
Debord, Guy 112
Decadence 38
decorative 7
Defries, Amelia 24, 33
Demuth, Charles 86
Dernière Mode, la 92, 93
Desnos, Robert 112, 115
'Destruction of Syntax' 45
Dickinson, Emily 29
Diderot, Denis 109
Dionysius 112
Dodge, Edwin 63, 69
Dodge, Mabel (Luhan) 8, 40, 54, 63, 64, 84, 104
Doucet, Jacques 109
Dresden china 70
Dresser, Arlene 86
Duchamp, Marcel ('Totor') 9, 84–8, 112–13, 116, 155
Dufy, Raoul 125
Duncan, Isadora 33
Duomo 61, 62
Duse, Eleonora 60

The Egoist 162
Eliot, T. S. (T. S. Apteryx) 162, 168
Emerson, Ralph Waldo 29
Epicure, The 189
Etoile de Mer 115
'Exodus' 14

fascism 38
First World War 40

Fiume 60
flabbergast fraternity 54
Flint, R. W. 37, 47
Florence 7, 8, 21, 30, 32, 37, 174
Fountain 84–5
France, French (Paris) 13, 84, 87, 104
Francophile 47
Frankel, Hans 18
Freytag-Loringhoven, Baroness Elsa von 80, 81, 83, 86
Futurism 8, 10, 12, 36–62, 32, 86, 102, 107, 120, 145

Gabinetto Vieusseuxs
  Gate Crushers of Olympus 70
  Gazette des Beaux-Arts 134
Germany, German 13, 20
Gide, André ('Androgide') 43, 110
Gothic 12, 134, 135
Grand Central Palace 8, 84
Grandjean, Nellie 110
Gray, Eileen 22
Greenaway, Kate 16
Guggenheim, Peggy 116, 138, 139
Gulf of Mexico 49
Guys, Constantin 134

Hale, Terry 104, 109
Haweis, Giles 33, 115
Haweis, Oda Janet 25, 30, 115
Haweis, Stephen 7, 21–33, 101, 115–16, 134
  Dusie (Mina Loy nude) 23
  Sea Garden 22
Heap, Jane 48, 89, 149
Herwick, Esther Jane 190
Hotel Druout 69

General Index

Hotel Jerome 188, 189
Hotel Lutétia 126
Hugo, Victor 48
hypochondria 14, 21

Independent Artists, Independent Exhibition 8, 9, 84
Italy, Italian 84

Jarry, Alfred 43
jazz 115–16

Kafka, Franz 124
Klemperer, Irene 170
Knight, Eva 21
Kreymborg, Alfred 76
  Lima Beans 142

Lacerba 37, 41, 47
Ladies' Journals 12
Lamba, Jacqueline 139
lampshades 116, 127
Laurencin, Marie 108
Le Savoureux, Henri Joël 7, 30
  photograph of Stephen Haweis and Mina Loy 134
Legree, Simon 125
Lethe 187
Level, André 92
Levertov, Denise 191
Levy, Julien 116
Lewis, Wyndham 38, 116
Little Review 57
London 10, 14, 16, 17, 22, 105, 107, 174
  Grove Road 17
  Hampstead 18
  St John's Wood 17

logopoeia 10, 68
Lowy family 14, 17, 21
  Dora and Hilda, Mina's sisters 21
Loy, Mina 19, 23, 29, 31, 32, 99, 114, 118, 119, 134, 139, 143, 144, 146, 147, 149, 185

McAlmon, Robert 89, 121
madness 106–7
Mafarka 66
Maintenant 92, 104, 109–10
Mallarmé, Stéphane 39, 42, 92, 170
Man Ray 107, 125, 145
  photograph of Mina Loy 146, 151
manifestos 44
Mannerism 12
Marinetti, Filippo Tommaso 8, 12, 36, 37–62, 88, 107
  'Battle of Adrianople' 38
Marmar, Sandeep 129
Marquis, Don 77
Marshall, Alan 112
Medici 64, 106–7
Merton, Thomas 191
Methodism 14, 16
Mexico 9, 91, 107, 112
Milan 8, 12, 37
Monroe, Harriet 121
Montparnasse, Kiki de 115
Moore, George 22
Moore, Marianne 12
Mucha, Alphonse 22
Munich 7, 14, 18, 20

Nadja (Léona Delcourt) 109
New York 8, 10, 12, 21, 102

Bowery 12, 13, 62, 72, 170, 187, 191
Bowery bums 12, 13, 123, 126, 177
Lower East Side 12
Third Avenue 172
neurasthenia 30
Nietzsche, Friedrich 29, 112
   Ecce homo 112
Norton, Louise 145
   'Dame Rogue's Philosophic
      Fashions' 145
   'Nowism', 'nunism' 102

Oelze 49, 122
Ouida 17

Paepke, Walter 180
Paget, Violet (Vernon Lee) 30
Pamperers, The 57, 69, 70, 84
Papini, Giovanni 8, 12, 30, 37–62,
   39
Paris 7, 17, 20, 21, 115, 174
Passatismo 38
Passion Play 20
Patini, Giovanni 33
Pessoa, Fernando 13, 51
Petit Larousse 93
Picabia, Francis 9, 88
Picasso, Pablo 47, 70–71
plumbing ('God') 86
Poesia 37, 43
Pound, Ezra 10, 17, 57, 68, 89, 110,
   121, 130
Pre-Raphaelities 17
Prescott, Tara 12
Protestantism 16
PTB (Roché, Duchamp, Wood) 86
Puerto Angel 9

Raffay, André, *Chez Arensberg* 82
Red Mountain 190
Rexroth, Kenneth 191
Rhodoid 117
Rimbaud, Arthur 109
Roché, Henri-Pierre 85, 89
Rodin, Auguste 22
Rogue 88
Rops, Félicien 134
Rossetti, Dante Gabriel 17
Russolo, Luigi 43
Rye, Jane 47

Sacred Prostitute, The 57, 69–70
Saint-Point, Valentine de 45
Salina Cruz 9, 92, 100
Salon d'automne 135
satire 10
Schamberg, Morton 86
Schiaparelli, Elsa 128
Schulman, Grace 178
Sebbag, Georges 109
Sheeler, Charles 88
Soffici, Ardenzo 41, 43, 48
spectacularity 68
Stein, Gertrude 8, 63, 64, 77, 88,
   117, 150
Stella, Joseph 80, 85
Stettheimer, Florine (conversation
   pictures) 89
Stevens, Wallace 88, 178
Stieglitz, Alfred, Stieglitz
   Gallery 88
Surrealism 10, 76, 122

tailor, draper 14
Taos 63
La Tarantella 69

General Index

Temple de l'Amitié 8
Thomson, Virgil 117
Tzara, Tristan (Sami Rosenstock) 149, 166–9
   L'Homme approximatif 167–9

Vaché, Jacques 109
Vail, Lawrence 138
Vallombrosa 54
Van Vechten, Carl 8, 40, 54, 57, 63, 145
Varèse, Edgard 87–8
Vas Diass, Robert 191
La Voce 41, 42, 43
Venice 38
Villa Curonia 64, 104

Vitalism 40, 65, 102
Weiss, Eric 110
Whistler, James Abbott McNeill 7, 22
Whitman, Walt 38
Wilde, Dolly ('Oscaria') 117
Wilde, Oscar 11, 30
Williams, Jonathan 188, 191
   photograph of Mina Loy in *Aspen* 185
Williams, William Carlos 144, 191
Wood, Beatrice 84–7, 87
   Mina Loy and Arthur Cravan 99
   Un peu d'eau dans du savon 87
   poster for the Blindman's Ball *141*